START A
SUCCESSFUL
BUSINESS

START A
SUCCESSFUL
BUSINESS

 **EXPERT ADVICE TO TAKE YOUR STARTUP FROM IDEA TO EMPIRE**

Colleen DeBaise

ΔAMACOM
AMERICAN MANAGEMENT ASSOCIATION

New York • Atlanta • Brussels • Chicago • Mexico City • San Francisco
Shanghai • Tokyo • Toronto • Washington, D. C.

Bulk discounts available. For details visit:
www.amacombooks.org/go/specialsales
Or contact special sales:
Phone: 800-250-5308
Email: specialsls@amanet.org
View all the AMACOM titles at: www.amacombooks.org
American Management Association: www.amanet.org

This publication is designed to provide accurate and authoritative information in regard to the subject matter covered. It is sold with the understanding that the publisher is not engaged in rendering legal, accounting, or other professional service. If legal advice or other expert assistance is required, the services of a competent professional person should be sought.

Library of Congress Cataloging-in-Publication Data

Names: DeBaise, Colleen, author.
Title: Start a successful business : expert advice to take your startup from
   idea to empire / Colleen DeBaise.
Description: New York : AMACOM, [2018] | Includes index. |
Identifiers: LCCN 2017039547 (print) | LCCN 2017041500 (ebook) | ISBN
   9780814439197 (ebook) | ISBN 9780814439180 (pbk.)
Subjects: LCSH: New business enterprises. | Strategic planning.
Classification: LCC HD62.5 (ebook) | LCC HD62.5 .D4213 2018 (print) | DDC
   658.1/1--dc23
LC record available at https://lccn.loc.gov/2017039547

About AMA

American Management Association (www.amanet.org) is a world leader in talent development, advancing the skills of individuals to drive business success. Our mission is to support the goals of individuals and organizations through a complete range of products and services, including classroom and virtual seminars, webcasts, webinars, podcasts, conferences, corporate and government solutions, business books, and research. AMA's approach to improving performance combines experiential learning—learning through doing—with opportunities for ongoing professional growth at every step of one's career journey.

10 9 8 7 6 5 4 3 2 1

>>>> **CONTENTS**

>>>> ACKNOWLEDGMENTS

WHEN WE SET OUT TO compile this book, we didn't have to search too far to find the best material.

For nearly forty years, *Inc.* has provided advice, education, and inspiration to the leaders of fast-growing private companies, chiefly through our unrivaled editorial content.

That material—produced by veteran reporters, all-star editors, and expert columnists, among others—is what you see on the pages of this book.

We have gathered some of the best *Inc.* insights, tips, and case studies and presented them in a single path-charting guide. Our thanks to the talented contributors whose work is reflected here. With the *Inc.* team on your side, starting a business will be faster, less confusing—and ultimately, more rewarding than you ever imagined.

T
HIS BOOK, CHOCK FULL OF inspirational startup stories, is designed to activate your best, most creative, most informed entrepreneurial self.

We're confident that it contains the "secret" to successful entrepreneurship—that special sauce that will help you turn your dream into a full-blown reality. Which isn't as closely guarded as you might think.

A word about us: We're the editors of *Inc.*, and for decades, we've interviewed the makers, doers, and dreamers who have launched some of America's most celebrated companies. You'll hear from many of them throughout this book.

Over the years, we've observed a consistent paradox as we sat down with entrepreneurs who have turned nuggets of ideas into global enterprises. These company builders come from all different walks of life, with varied levels of expertise or education, and they take markedly divergent paths as they start and grow their startups. Yet somehow, they all manage to end up in the same place: On top.

How do they do it? The answer is that they know the recipe for entrepreneurial success, that strange combination of inspired action, calculated risk, and hard work that isn't necessarily taught in any business school class. They've figured out the "secret."

Which brings us to you. Chances are, if you've picked up this book, you're thinking about taking that leap. But you're hesitating to do so because—well, nothing makes sense about it. Maybe you've got a corporate job with perks and benefits. Maybe you've got student loan debt. Maybe you've got a young family. Maybe you've got plenty of skills or expertise in one area, but not enough in others.

And maybe—most naggingly—you just don't know *how* to do it. You can envision your product or service (whatever it is) on store shelves, or on mobile devices, or in people's homes, stomachs, or offices worldwide. But you just don't know how to get from point A to point B.

If any of those apply to you, then congrats! You're like most aspiring entrepreneurs. The difference between you and the celebrated ones is that they've gone ahead and navigated the rocky terrain connecting point A to point B. They know the way. At *Inc.*, our reporters and editors have observed the patterns that have emerged, the twists and turns those entrepreneurs have taken along the way, and we're revealing them to you in the pages ahead.

This book will walk you through seven crucial stages that we've identified as key to taking your startup from idea to empire. Give it a read, and absorb it. We hope our guide gives you the knowledge to make your decision, the confidence to stick to your plan, and the tools to help you succeed beyond your wildest dreams.

COME UP WITH A BRILLIANT BUSINESS IDEA

> ❝ We couldn't sleep, because we thought it was such a good idea."

—

NEIL BLUMENTHAL, co-founder of online eyewear company Warby Parker.

SURE, YOU WANT TO BE an empire maker. But first you need an idea. A really good one. Some might say brilliant.

Startup ideas can come from just about anywhere—truly. Let's look at the most common sources:

→ A theme or problem from your daily life

→ An emerging trend

→ A gap in a specific market

→ A drive to help others in an inventive way

→ A special skill or expertise that you possess

Which is best? We've asked scores of successful entrepreneurs and noted experts this very same question. And far and away, they agree: It's that first one, the problem or "pain point" that you personally experience on a regular basis, that is the ideal motivation for starting a company.

While you can (and should) pull from any of the sources on the above list for your startup idea, it's wise to draw primarily from your own need or frustration. Why, exactly? Starting a company will require long hours and seemingly endless focus. Both are much easier when you feel a personal connection to the purpose behind the company.

> **"** The advice I have for entrepreneurs is... number one, you need to solve a real problem. I look for those problems in my own life. Mint was because I had a challenge managing my own finances using Quicken and Microsoft Money. So I built it for myself."
>
> **AARON PATZER,** founder of web-based personal finance service Mint.com, which he ultimately sold to Intuit for $170 million

If you don't have that burning, personal desire to see your concept come to fruition, we don't recommend pursuing your startup idea.

That's because the early days of starting a company are notoriously difficult. You might find yourself questioning whether you've made the right call. That's especially true as the months or years drag on, and you've decided to quit a lucrative career, invest personal savings, and sacrifice time away from family to chase your dream. (Many seasoned entrepreneurs, by the way, say it takes at least three years to find your startup footing, and that many newbies give up too soon.)

But beyond that, there's another reason why it makes sense to let your personal challenge lead the way. Chances are, others are experiencing the same problem as well—even if they're not entirely aware of it. They're called your customers.

> " I spent all my hard-earned money on this one pair of cream pants that hung there, and I decided to cut the feet out of control top pantyhose one day, and I threw them on under my white pants, and went to the party. I looked fabulous, I felt great, I had no panty lines, I looked thinner and smoother... and I remember thinking, "This should exist for women."
>
> **SARA BLAKELY,** inventor of Spanx underwear, whose net worth is now valued at more than $1 billion

Of course, you might say to yourself: "Wait a minute. Yes, this is a personal frustration of mine. And others probably experience it as well. But chances are, someone else is already working on a solution."

Guess what: You're exactly right. In some form or another, nearly every idea is already out there. But how you implement your idea, position your new concept, and execute your plan can be the defining factor of success.

Countless billion-dollar companies are based on ideas that were just tweaks of what was there before. Facebook, for example, is far from an original idea. Social networks had been around for nearly a decade, in companies such as SixDegrees, Friendster, and Myspace. Facebook's success didn't come from the idea itself but instead from countless iterations around how the product could reach customers and achieve a competitive advantage.

"Every company needs a starting point," says Eric Paley, managing partner of seed-stage venture capital fund Founder Collective. "I encourage entrepreneurs to focus more on falling in love with the problems they want to solve rather than their initial ideas."

As founders dig deeply into that original hypothesis, they will learn, adapt, hit walls, adapt again, and build critical expertise that they never considered when starting out. "In fact, in many cases the original idea later seems humorous or at least incredibly naive compared with the lengths to which the startup needs to go to become successful," Paley says.

Readers who are old enough might recall when Jeff Bezos launched Amazon.com in 1994 as a bookseller. Or when Reed Hastings co-founded Netflix in 1997 as a DVD rental service. Both have transformed their companies into something very different than their original concepts.

It's important to remember that the startup you first set out to build will not resemble the company you are operating five or ten years later. Startups, and businesses in general, evolve and take on lives of their own—in large part due to technological advances or changing customer tastes.

The most successful entrepreneurs always keep a finger on the pulse of the current market (more on that in Chapter 5). After launching, they ask questions such as "How is the product performing?" "Is it easy or hard to sell?" "What kind of value does the product provide in the current climate?" "Is it generating revenue or not?"

> **"** A vision…is the most powerful and unique asset any company has. The original idea for my company started out of a simple pain point I wanted to fix: Find a [fitness] class easily. As ClassPass grew, my vision expanded further into making fitness a way of life. We've pivoted our company a few times, and the most important reason was because it didn't map to our true north. It's hard to always predict how customers will engage with your product; when you see a behavior that isn't aligned to your vision, you have to be able to shift gears. Ultimately, your vision has to be at the core of everything you do, even if that means adjusting or iterating your product roadmap to make sure you get there."

PAYAL KADAKIA, founder of fitness startup ClassPass, a.k.a. the "Netflix for workout classes," which has shifted its business model, raised prices, and discontinued its popular-but-unsustainable unlimited workout option, all since launching in 2013

Based on all that, you might find it tricky to come up with a brilliant business idea, particularly if you understand that your startup will need to keep changing and iterating. That's why some entrepreneurs also recommend coming up with a vision, which stays true even as your company morphs.

FINDING YOUR NICHE

The best business ideas come from your strongest areas of interest, says Ryan Robinson, an entrepreneur and writer who teaches people how to create self-employed careers.

When the going gets rough (and it will), you need to be motivated beyond just the lure of dollar signs. If you're only in it for the money, you'll either give up or be quickly pushed out of the market by people who genuinely care about what they're doing and the people they're helping—they'll be more motivated than you.

If you're not sure what your interests are, or which of them may potentially lead to a profitable business opportunity, ask yourself the following questions. The answers may help you find your way.

- → What are your hobbies?

- → What is the most meaningful part of your day?

- → What are some topics you could enjoy writing a thousand-word article about?

- → What do you love doing?

→ What is an achievement that'd make you feel particularly proud of yourself?

→ Are there any specific aspects or functions that you love about your current job?

→ How about any childhood dreams you still find intriguing?

→ If you had to choose just one thing to be remembered by, what would it be?

Money Makers

When mulling your business ideas, it's always wise to consider where your idea fits in the general marketplace. For instance, in 2017 *Inc.* interviewed experts and examined investment data to find the industries that are beginning to offer major opportunities for new ventures. Here are the ones that held the most promise.

- **Meditation and mindfulness training.** Increased corporate spending on programs to improve employee focus has helped boost an industry that research firm IBISWorld values at $1.1 billion in the United States. App-based training is bringing the practice to an even broader audience.

- **Ready-to-drink coffee and tea.** Consumers are ditching mixes and concentrates in favor of on-the-go coffee and tea, largely driven by health innovations. From 2013 to 2015, U.S. sales of these drinks nearly tripled, landing at $143 million, according to the nonprofit Specialty Food Association.

- **Mobility tech.** This industry offers startups potential partnerships with and acquisition by large tech companies and automakers working on autonomous vehicles. Ford, for example, invested $1 billion in Pittsburgh-based Argo AI in its effort to develop a self-driving car by 2021.

- **Pet care.** Tech innovations are making over this industry, which is valued at $60 billion in the United States. Revenue for pet grooming and boarding alone was nearly $8 billion in the United States. in 2016, according to IBISWorld, which projects it to grow 7 percent annually through 2021.

- **Construction management.** Global funding for hardware and software to streamline building projects, or to sell and rent construction equipment, rose to $254 million in 2015 from $51 million in 2010, according to researcher CB Insights—and analysts say it's still an emerging industry.

- **Synthetic biology**. Health and environmental concerns have driven interest in genetically engineered medicines, foods, and fuel. It's a costly and technical field, but payoffs can be huge for companies like DNA manufacturing company Twist Bioscience.

- **Computer vision.** Advancements in artificial intelligence have produced companies working to interpret and act on visual data. The technology, which attracted $522 million and 69 deals in 2016, can be applied to child development, social media networks, and web analytics.

- **Brick-and-mortar retail technology.** Startups are helping modernize in-store operations. One notable example is London-based Iconeme, which created technology that pushes product information from mannequins to nearby shoppers' smartphones.

NEXT STEPS:
GET FEEDBACK

Once you've pinpointed a pain point and settled on a vision, it's time to start finessing your startup idea. The best way to do that is to seek outside perspectives. In other words, it's time to hash it out with anyone who will listen. (For more on that, see "Building a Personal Team of Advisors," page 14.) That list includes:

→ Friends and family

→ Work colleagues (including former co-workers or bosses)

→ Classmates or professors

→ Members of networking groups that you belong to

→ Fellow entrepreneurs

→ Potential customers

We know exactly what you're thinking: "But what if someone steals my amazing idea?"

Guess what: Ideas, even the brilliant ones, are worth very little. Unfortunately, too many aspiring entrepreneurs become fixated on the value of their big ideas, declining to speak with others who might provide advice or feedback. They believe sharing an idea with other people will hurt them. This is a terrible mistake.

> ❝ For several years, I worked closely with a brilliant inventor named Natan Parsons, who had almost a hundred patents under his belt and invented the mechanism behind automatic flush toilets. He would always solicit feedback about products he had in the works from prospective customers. He'd tell people what he was doing, but not how—and it was the "how" that he patented.
>
> Remember: If sharing your idea gives away all its value, it's probably not a defensible idea to begin with."
>
> **ROBERT GLAZER,** serial entrepreneur whose digital marketing firm, Acceleration Partners, works with brands that include Adidas, Bonobos, and ModCloth

When you're thinking about launching a new product or service—particularly one that is unlike anything else on the market—it's critical to talk to others to understand potential customers' needs and to gauge their feedback. The worst thing you can do, many experts say, is to operate in stealth mode. While you may *think* you need a patent, most experts say your limited resources are better spent on developing your business idea.

Patents can offer value to companies. For example, venture capital investors might insist on them. They can give an entrepreneur the legal standing to demand redress from someone who encroaches on the patent...assuming that the entrepreneur has the money to litigate the case and can come to a contingency arrangement with a qualified law firm.

But, if you have limited funds, getting to market and creating revenue are more important steps. There are other ways to stymie competitors. A better product, smarter marketing, better customer service, and more effective business processes are just a few examples of how to get ahead of other companies.

John D. Smith, an inventor and entrepreneur, wrote a book called *Don't File a Patent!*, which comes from his experience developing and selling a hurricane window protection device. He had filed other patents successfully, and tried to patent the hurricane window, but the U.S. Patent & Trademark Office rejected the patent three times. The conclusion he reached was that he had spent "almost $25,000 in legal and government filing fees" to no useful end. He says that he would have been better off putting the money into selling the product.

If you truly need a patent, you can always begin the process at a later date. You have up to one year from when your invention is first made public (by being announced or put on sale) in which to patent it, according to Minda Zeltin, coauthor of *The Geek Gap*. "And you can always file a provisional patent application, something like a save-the-date note for a wedding," she says. It doesn't commit you to a formal patent application, and doesn't result in a patent, but it does allow you to claim your invention so that you can do a full patent application later. For more information, including answers to frequently asked questions about patents, visit the USPTO's site at www.uspto.gov.

Building a Personal Team of Advisors

It's never too early in your entrepreneurial career to surround yourself with good people.

"Many of us are convinced that we have to fly solo and figure everything out on our own, the hard way—that having a support team and advisors is only for the powerful or wildly successful," says Antonio Neves, a leadership speaker and former TV journalist. "This is foolish and naive. You don't have to do it alone. In fact, you shouldn't."

People are more willing to help us accomplish our goals than we may think, according to Neves. "In fact, they want to help," he says. "The hard, challenging, and vulnerable part is this: It's our job to ask for their help."

Neves recommends that newbie entrepreneurs form a "personal" board of advisors—a small but important group of professionals or experts that guide decision making and provide critical input and advice. To find them, he recommends listing the areas where you'll likely need additional help and expertise (e.g., fundraising, marketing, design, etc.). Then, evaluate your network—LinkedIn connections, Facebook friends, current or former professors, family friends, etc.—to see who could fill the void in your gap areas.

Next, ask for an informational meeting with your potential advisor. Explain what you're doing and why you're seeking their help, as well as what type of support you need from them and what this might look like (such as weekly, bi-weekly, or monthly calls). "Once someone agrees to become your advisor, always treat this relationship with the utmost care, tact, and professionalism," he says. "Be generous with your 'thank yous' and create as much value for them as possible."

NEXT STEPS:
GATHER INFORMATION
ABOUT YOUR TARGET MARKET

Large corporations with big budgets routinely conduct market research to see if it's worthwhile to launch a new product or service. The good news is that gauging customer sentiment doesn't need to be expensive, according to Inc.com columnist Christina DesMarais. There are plenty of informal ways to figure out whether there's potential demand for your idea and, if so, who your customer might be or what your market size might be:

→ **Turn an industry event into a research venue.** Attend a trade show or conference in your chosen field, which should give you an opportunity to talk with your target audience. Find out who will be attending and schedule face-to-face time with these people, if only for a few minutes.

→ **Try social media to crowdsource your research.** Pose a few targeted questions to your potential fan base on Facebook, Instagram, Twitter, or LinkedIn. It may not be the most robust research, and your audience may be biased, but it's a good way to get simple questions answered.

→ **Use do-it-yourself tools, such as SurveyMonkey, to get quick and simple feedback.** Or gather a few people for a real-life focus group. Start small: You don't need to talk to thousands of people if twenty or thirty will give you a good idea what direction to head.

→ **Consider a crowdfunding campaign.** Yes, this is a fairly work-intensive way to raise early-stage funds (more on finding money for your business in Chapter 3). But it's also a technique to gauge whether strangers and your network are interested in your product or service. The most popular sites are Kickstarter and Indiegogo, and the most successful campaigns include pitch videos.

→ **Find what's already out there.** You may be surprised what you can learn by searching the Internet for existing studies. For example, a wealth of data exists on millennial consumers, such as how they like to be engaged, what social networks they use, and more. While the research you find may not be specific to your industry, you're wasting money if you're asking questions that have already been answered.

Lastly, don't forget to log all your customer input. Any kind of feedback you're getting—whether in person, through your emails, or via social networks—should be captured, so you can better study customer problems, habits, and lifestyles.

Rent the Runway

IN 2009, JENNIFER HYMAN and Jennifer Fleiss launched Rent the Runway, a website that allows customers to rent designer gowns and accessories at a fraction of the retail price.

The co-founders came up with the idea while students at Harvard Business School. The two had witnessed young women, including Hyman's sister Becky, agonize over what to wear to weddings and other events, despite having a closet full of clothes. "We realized there was a real gap in rationality around fashion, where woman constantly want new things," often when they have limited budgets, Fleiss says. "Wouldn't there be a great opportunity—rather than buying a fast-fashion knock-off—to get the actual designer dress through a rental model, where you only keep it for a day or two?"

Hyman and Fleiss decided to see if the idea had merit. The two bought hundreds of dresses at Bloomingdale's (mostly in their size, as they figured they'd at least have fantastic wardrobes if things didn't work out). "We first tested out our idea by going to Harvard with a trunk full of dresses that we let girls try on and rent. Next, we went to Yale and rented out the dresses but didn't let women try them on," Fleiss says. "For the third trial, we sent out a PDF to students that said, 'Call us if you want to rent this dress.' Each time, we were getting closer and closer to what our actual concept was—an Internet dress-rental site—to prove that it was really going to work."

Fleiss estimates that they talked to thousands of young women before launching. "A big mistake that many entrepreneurs make is being hesitant to share information about their concept with others," Fleiss says. "Jenn and I did the exact opposite. We shared our idea with as many designers, women, and investors as we possibly could and utilized their feedback to tweak our original idea."

Fleiss adds that it was particularly important to talk to potential customers, as renting designer gowns via the Internet (at that time) was a new, disruptive concept. "We knew we needed to test our idea on the ground to see if we could actually promote 'renting' as a new consumer behavior," she says.

Getting outside perspectives paid off. Today, Rent the Runway has annual revenue of over $100 million. The company has raised more than $190 million in venture capital, and is opening brick-and-mortar locations in New York, Los Angeles, and other cities.

—

Summarize Your Idea

During the early stages, you'll want to come up with a short description of your idea that you could share with anyone (and get even more feedback). This can ultimately become your "elevator pitch," a succinct and memorable recitation of what makes you special, which ideally resonates with the heart and the mind of your listener.

For the unfamiliar, the concept is simple: If you happen to find yourself on an elevator with an investor or customer, you can communicate what you do in the short time (20 to 60 seconds) it takes to ride from the ground floor to your destination.

"While the elevator scenario is a bit absurd, there's no question that chance conversations can result in business opportunities," says Inc.com columnist Geoffrey James, author of *Business Without the Bullsh*t*, a book about essential business skills. "The CEO of one of the largest credit card processors in the United States once told me how he sold the idea for his new business to an investor whom he met at a wedding."

James offers the following advice on what your "elevator pitch" should contain: A carefully crafted sentence (that's just one sentence, folks) that describes who you are and what you do. If your listener is interested, then proceed to explain why you and your startup are unique and different from the competition. Reveal one or two facts that prove your uniqueness.

Most people, by the way, confuse elevator pitches with sales pitches, but they're completely different. "A sales pitch is a formal presentation," he says. "An elevator pitch is a segue that takes place within a casual conversation." Most typically, you use an elevator pitch when you run into a potential customer or investor at a conference, trade show, or social event.

NEXT STEPS:
ANALYZE COMPETITION;
FIGURE OUT YOUR ADVANTAGE

" If you don't have a competitive advantage, don't compete."

—
JACK WELCH, former chairman and CEO of General Electric

It's also wise to scope out the competition while you're still forming your idea. (And here's where you'll likely discover that you're not the only person with this fabulous concept.) This is especially important if you want to tap into a crowded marketplace, where there are plenty of customers and many players—or a few dominant ones— willing to serve them.

A competitive advantage, by definition, is that unique edge that allows your business to attract more customers or achieve greater sales than rivals. In essence, it's what makes your business, your business. And it can mean the difference between being an also-ran and leading the pack.

Your competitive advantage can come in many forms, including:

→ Your prices

→ Distinct or high-quality products

→ Your distribution network

→ Customer service

→ Your own personal skill set, experience, or industry knowledge

→ Strategic relationships or partnerships

> **❝** In business, you have only two ways of surviving: Either your product is better than your competitors', or it's cheaper. There's simply no other foundation on which to build a successful business. None. Better or cheaper, take your pick."
>
> —
>
> **JIM KOCH,** founder of Boston Beer Co., which now has a market cap of $1.7 billion

One way to identify your competitive advantage is to take a look at the early feedback that you've obtained from outsiders or from your target audience. See if any patterns, trends, or commonalities emerge. Consider those themes to be potential "value propositions" as you continue to develop your idea.

While competitive advantage can be cut-and-dry for some entrepreneurs, others find it tricky to put their finger on. Some companies, in fact, take years to identify what truly makes them stand out. We recommend identifying your competitive advantage as soon as possible, so you nurture that advantage and effectively use it in marketing.

Famed Harvard economist Michael E. Porter wrote the landmark book *Competitive Strategy* in 1980, offering the "five forces" model to determine your unique advantage. While much has changed since 1980, Porter's analytical tools are still useful for anyone pursuing a new product or service. His view is that these five forces shape every industry, and can help you determine your strengths and weaknesses:

1. **Threat of new entrants.** How easily could new competitors enter your space? Do others face significant barriers, such as large capital requirements or government regulation?

2. **Threat of substitute products or services.** How readily could customers bypass you with other options? If you make aluminum windows, for instance, you need to worry about makers of vinyl windows.

3. **Bargaining power of customers.** How much leeway do you have, in terms of pricing? If your customers are a lot more powerful than you, they may beat you down on price or force you to provide free services.

4. **Bargaining power of suppliers.** How much relative power do suppliers have to set prices and conditions for doing business? If you are dependent on specialty suppliers or one or two dominant vendors, you will have to pay whatever they ask.

5. **Intensity of competitive rivalry.** How many powerful competitors operate in your space? Competition can be civil and subdued, or it can be vicious and warlike.

In a column for *Inc.*, Porter says entrepreneurs can follow three basic strategies when it comes to achieving a competitive advantage and creating profits.

1. **You can have consistently lower costs than your rivals.** "As long as your product maintains an acceptable quality level, that will lead to higher margins," he says.

2. **You can differentiate your product or service from your competitors.** "That allows you to command a premium price," he says. "And provided you keep your costs under control, the premium price will translate into a superior return."

3. **You can position yourself in terms of scope.** "Some companies seek advantage in what might be called a broad scope: They serve more or less all types of customers in an industry," he says. By contrast, "companies with a narrow scope...dedicate all their efforts to one small niche or mar-

ket segment." In cars, for example, Toyota is a broad, low-cost competitor, while BMW and Mercedes-Benz target the narrower premium segment.

The worst error, by far, is failing to choose any of these—price, differentiation, or scope—and "therefore not have any advantage at all," he says. "That is what I call 'stuck in the middle.'"

Warby Parker

IN FEBRUARY 2008, FOUR MBA candidates at the Wharton School of business wondered: Why weren't eyeglasses sold online, for a heck of a lot cheaper than in stores? It wasn't a completely random thought. One of them, Neil Blumenthal, had run a nonprofit called VisionSpring that trains women in the developing world to give eye exams and sell glasses.

"Why are glasses so expensive? I've personally been to the factories," Blumenthal says. "I've known that they didn't cost that much to manufacture. What were keeping prices so high in the U.S.?"

Blumenthal and the others (Dave Gilboa, Andy Hunt, and Jeff Raider) began investigating. "What we found is this industry is dominated by a few large companies that are keeping prices artificially high," he says. Italian company Luxottica, for instance, pretty much owns the eyewear business, controlling 80 percent of the industry through brands that include Prada, Ray-Ban, and even Sunglass Hut and Lenscrafters. After realizing that, the four begin thinking: "We could come in and disrupt and charge one-fourth of what they're charging—and hopefully begin to take market share," according to Blumenthal.

And with that, a business model featuring a significant competitive advantage was born. Two years later, the four launched WarbyParker.com, selling prescription glasses for $95—far cheaper than brick-and-mortar competitors who typically charged upwards of $500.

Today, Warby Parker is worth more than $1 billion. The company has always differentiated itself by selling online—it lets customers select up to five styles of eyeglasses online and have them delivered to their homes to test out for free. (Warby Parker has since expanded to 46 retail locations, too.) Blumenthal believes that the Netflix-type model allows the company to handle shifting consumer preferences better than its competitors.

One unique advantage: It has attracted millennial consumers, who like to support socially conscious companies, with a one-for-one charity model. Warby Parker pledges to donate a pair of glasses to those in need for every pair sold. To date, Warby Parker has donated more than two million pairs of glasses.

—

A FEW LAST WORDS:
A LOOK AT THE ENTREPRENEURIAL MINDSET

As you move forward with your idea, you might ask yourself: Do I have what it takes to be an entrepreneur? And what, exactly, sets the best entrepreneurs apart from the pack?

Those are good questions...so good that a few years ago, *Inc.* staff writer Leigh Buchanan decided to examine them as we prepared the Inc. 500, our annual ranking of America's fastest-growing private companies. She noticed companies on the list were achieving impressive acceleration *without* tailwinds from the overall economy.

"We talk about the Inc. 500 as a collection of elite companies, but what this ranking really honors is a collection of elite entrepreneurs," Buchanan writes. More than 90 percent of Inc. 500 CEOs are also their companies' founders. The majority are serial entrepreneurs; about one-fifth started their first business before age twenty.

"These people are, by their own proud declarations, 'unemployable,'" she writes. "But not in the sense that other companies don't want them. Only in the sense that other companies can't contain them."

Yet when *Inc.* asked these entrepreneurs what made them successful, nearly three-quarters attributed their accomplishments to luck. "We're not buying it," Buchanan continues. "We've always assumed the leaders of America's fastest-growing companies were not merely in the right place at the right time with the right resume. Rather, we've believed them to be disproportionately gifted with the talents needed to build businesses."

We invited our Inc. 500 leaders to complete the Entrepreneurial StrengthsFinder assessment, a tool developed by Gallup, the global research firm. Some 150 did so. Gallup then compared the results with those from a national sample of close to 2,700 entrepreneurs. In every dimension, the Inc. 500 leaders scored higher. "In some cases, Everest-versus-Rushmore higher," Buchanan writes.

Gallup found that Inc. 500 founders were more than twice as likely as the national sample to score high on all ten entrepreneurial strengths. Inc. 500 founders also proved themselves multi-trick ponies, on average scoring high on six of the ten strengths. The national sample scored high on just two. Sixteen percent of Inc. 500 CEOs earned scores high enough to be classified as exceptional by Gallup, compared with 2 percent in the national sample.

The Inc. 500 entrepreneurs excel in every area identified by Gallup. But they absolutely dominate in three strengths—risk-taking, business focus, and determination—compared with the national sample. Those strengths are, not coincidentally, the ones most universally associated with business starts, survival, and scaling.

The group's top-ranked talent is risk-taking—"which will surprise nobody," Buchanan says. "After all, without risk there is no business." To launch their companies, the entrepreneurs were willing to sacrifice everything, from parents' retirement funds to cushy executive perches. The Inc. 500 is packed with risk-takers walking away from six-figure salaries and taking on debt—often with young families in tow to sharpen the edge.

Gallup says those with a talent for risk-taking possess a highly optimistic perception of risk but are also rational decision makers who have an extraordinary ability to mitigate that risk. The assessment

PORTRAIT OF THE NOT-SO-AVERAGE INC. 500 CEO

Gallup compared the scores of 2,700 entrepreneurs on 10 crucial personality traits with those of Inc. 500 CEOs. Below is the percentage of each group that scored "high" on those traits, showcasing the overwhelming talent it takes to make the list.

● INC. 500 ENTREPRENEURS   ● NATIONAL SAMPLE ENTREPRENEURS

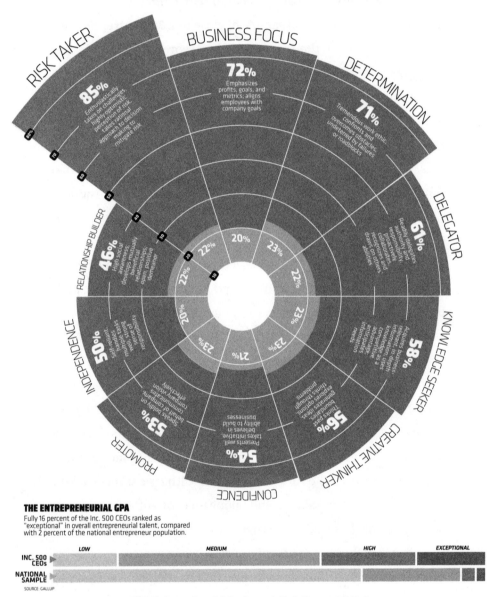

RISK TAKER
85%
Enthusiastically takes on challenges; highly optimistic perception of risk; takes rational approach to decision making to mitigate risk

BUSINESS FOCUS
72%
Emphasizes profits, goals, and metrics; aligns employees with company goals

DETERMINATION
71%
Tremendous work ethic; confronts and overcomes obstacles; undeterred by failures or roadblocks

DELEGATOR
61%
Readily delegates authority and responsibility; proactively collaborates; recognizes and draws on others' abilities

KNOWLEDGE SEEKER
58%
Acquires business relevant information; interest in depth knowledge; uses competitive advantage as a anticipates information needs

CREATIVE THINKER
56%
Thinks past boundaries; generates ideas; explores options; thinks through problems

CONFIDENCE
54%
Presents well; takes initiative; believes in ability to build businesses

PROMOTER
53%
Speaks boldly on behalf of company; communicates company vision effectively

INDEPENDENCE
50%
Self-reliant; handles tasks multiple tasks well; strong sense of responsibility

RELATIONSHIP BUILDER
46%
High social awareness; develops mutually beneficial relationships; open, positive demeanor

Inner ring values: 22%, 20%, 23%, 22%, 23%, 23%, 21%, 20%, 22%

THE ENTREPRENEURIAL GPA

Fully 16 percent of the Inc. 500 CEOs ranked as "exceptional" in overall entrepreneurial talent, compared with 2 percent of the national entrepreneur population.

	LOW	MEDIUM	HIGH	EXCEPTIONAL
INC. 500 CEOs ▶				
NATIONAL SAMPLE ▶				

SOURCE: GALLUP

SOURCE: Inc. media and Gallup Strengthsfinder Assessment Tool

shows that Inc. 500 founders are more likely than other entrepreneurs to take more and bigger risks. But they are also more likely to optimize their chances for good outcomes and, consequently, for rapid growth.

"As a company grows, so do the risks," Buchanan writes. "More is at stake—a business with a beating heart." And without business focus and determination, the Inc. 500 CEOs' second- and third-ranked strengths, a company can't survive and scale.

Gallup defines business focus as an emphasis on profit, goals, and metrics; basically, viewing decisions through a will-this-make-us-money lens. According to Gallup, the most talented Inc. 500 leaders were about 54 percent more likely to exceed their profit goals than the most talented leaders in the national sample.

So, while a typical company leader might hold weekly or monthly executive team meetings to discuss metrics, many business-focused Inc. 500 leaders report meeting daily to dissect every data point and adjust accordingly. At one company, Touchsuite, a seller of point-of-sale technology in Boca Raton, Florida, every lunch hour is devoted to the numbers. New goals are set monthly, and quarterly goals are chosen on the basis of a thorough analysis of maximum tangible impact. The team reevaluates three-to-five-year goals annually.

"Those practices speak to focus and discipline," Buchanan says. Gallup describes determination, the third-ranked talent, in terms of work ethic and the drive to achieve. The 500 are an unusually driven bunch. Ninety-seven percent of high-scoring Inc. 500 entrepreneurs said they intend to grow significantly.

Gallup also associates determination with a high "adversity quotient." Highly determined entrepreneurs have the ability to overcome obstacles and persevere despite failure. "That rings true," Buchanan says. "We have rarely interviewed an Inc. 500 founder who hasn't experienced a 'dark night of the soul.'"

Bernadette Coleman endured a very dark night in 2011, starting with the news that her son, Michael, was in a coma following a car crash. At the time, Advice Interactive Group, Coleman's Internet marketing company, based in McKinney, Texas, was just getting past its wobbly-fawn stage. For months, Coleman and her husband, Tom, the company's CFO, ran Advice Interactive from Michael's bedside and the stairwells of a Florida hospital. When performance lapses in the leaderless office threatened accounts, the couple redoubled their efforts. When half the staff quit—several to launch a competing business—the couple took turns flying back to Texas to hire replacements and run the company. "We were fighting for our son's life and for the company," says Coleman. "We had no choice but to prevail at both." Advice Interactive has appeared repeatedly on the Inc. 500, with revenue up more than 1,400 percent since the family's annus horribilis.

All of the Inc. 500 leaders' powers are great, but it seems their superpowers are largely concentrated in one area—45 percent have an "activation" or forceful style, where they make things happen (compared with 29 percent in the national sample). The finding makes sense, as the list tracks growth rates. "The more force you apply to something, the faster it accelerates," Buchanan says.

By comparison, the Inc. 500 CEOs are much softer on the soft skills. Only 16 percent have a relational style, compared with 40 percent for the national sample. And relationship-building turned up more often in the national sample's top three strengths than in the

Inc. 500's top three strengths. In fact, relationship-building is the one strength in which Inc. 500 founders scored below—though not far below—the seventy-fifth percentile.

Gallup describes relationship builders as having high social awareness, building mutually beneficial relationships, and getting to know customers and employees outside of work. "Of all the strengths, relationship-building takes the most time and patience, and the payoff is rarely immediate," Buchanan writes. That may explain why the action- and achievement-oriented Inc. 500 leaders lag behind in this area.

Relationship-building is considered a feminine trait, leadership studies show. Just 10 percent of Inc. 500 companies are led by women—a number that is growing, but still low.

Entrepreneurs with action-oriented talents may want to hire and develop women and men with "softer strengths" who are makers of friends and influencers of people, Buchanan concludes. That way, they can continue to rack up extraordinary gains and successes.

MIKE FELDMAN IS A "creative thinker," one of the key entrepreneurial strengths identified by Gallup's research. When Feldman first saw an iPhone, he did not think, *I should build an app for that!* Instead, he thought, *This technology is great, but it isolates people. I should come up with something that would bring people together.* Feldman's company, T1Visions, creates large-format touchscreens that let people in stores, classrooms, and offices share photos, play games, and collaborate. How did he test the product? By starting his own restaurant (a small tapas place) and embedding giant touchscreens in the tables and walls.

● ● ●

CLAYTON MOBLEY IS A "risk-taker." For the first four years that Mobley ran Spartan Value Investors, in Birmingham, Alabama, the company bought and resold foreclosed homes to consumers, with annual growth of 80 percent to 150 percent. Then, Mobley figured the company could quadruple revenue and profits by selling rental properties to investors and managing those properties for the new owners. Switching markets would require retraining 75 percent of staff, increasing monthly marketing expenses from nothing to $20,000, developing new services such as property management, and investing 60 percent of capital. Failure to execute would likely close Spartan's doors.

Mobley spent nine months studying the new industry. He was away so often doing research that vendors thought he had left the company. At last, he pulled the trigger. As a result, Spartan grew its revenue by over 800 percent. "You do everything you can to stay objective and make the right decision," says Mobley. "But at the end of the day, you have to make a bet on yourself."

● ● ●

MARIE FORLEO IS A relationship builder.

Forleo is the founder of New York City–based Marie Forleo International (2013 revenue: $11.9 million), which offers entrepreneurship and personal-development programs online. She has found not only jobs but also clients and employees while working in some of the most people-person jobs imaginable: bartender, fitness instructor, and life coach. She is forever introducing people to others who might help them, and being introduced in turn. Her relationships have won her invitations to appear on Oprah Winfrey's and Tony Robbins's programs, and her philanthropic work garnered her an invitation to travel to South Africa with Richard Branson.

"Every relationship that has helped me is the result of a from-the-heart, honest connection with someone I know and like," says Forleo. "That's where all the good things in life come from."

LAST WORDS:
WHY YOU SHOULDN'T FEAR FAILURE

❝ I spot winners by looking for somebody who went out and tried a business by him- or herself and maybe failed several times, but still has that determination, that love, and that passion for the company. It's very important to me that somebody has failed."

—

DAYMOND JOHN, Fubu founder and star of ABC's *Shark Tank*

We've talked about things that are preventing you from starting up, whether that's a hard-to-quit cushy corporate job, or a hard-to-shake uncertainty over whether you've really nailed down your brilliant idea.

Chances are, what might be really holding you back the most (whether you admit it or not) is a fear of failure.

But look around. Smart people say we should all fail, fast and often.

In fact, one argument is that failure can be the best teacher. "The benefits of a mistake can be greater than the costs. Failure is simply a departure from expectations," says Paul Schoemaker, author of *Brilliant Mistakes*, which challenges the negative stigma often attached to mistakes and failure. "Basically, it's the world telling you that you didn't see things in the best way to begin with."

Failure is sometimes heralded as the foundation of innovation. Mistakes allow for variation far beyond what was expected—you make a wrong turn, but ultimately find a better road to your destination. Thanks to mistakes, we now have such medical innovations as penicillin, smallpox vaccine, pacemakers, Viagra, and many others, according to the book *Happy Accidents* by author Morton Meyers.

And if you think about it, there's nothing *new* about failure in business, writes *Inc.* reporter Eric Markowitz. "In fact, failure is probably the constant of modern commerce: Companies are launched, they exist for a period of time, and then, well, they pretty much all fail."

These days Silicon Valley—that legendary breeding ground of entrepreneurs—loves failures, and for good reason.

Why? The most obvious answer is that failure has become inexpensive. Decades ago, starting a business typically entailed borrowing capital from a bank, friends, or family. Opening a physical storefront required lots of capital. Today, the Internet has democratized the process for starting up—building a website and hosting its data, even for e-commerce, are relatively inexpensive.

And while the web has made it easier and cheaper to start up and succeed, it has also made it easier and cheaper to fail.

"Simply put, the risk of failure is dramatically lower than it used to be," says Brian O'Malley, a general partner at Battery Ventures, a Silicon Valley venture capital firm. "With cloud services and new frameworks, something that used to take $10 million to test out can now be launched for $200,000. This makes it far easier for investors to take risks on unproven ideas and unproven teams."

Erica Zidel, who started an online babysitting co-op with her husband in 2011, says the Valley's embracing of failure has a lot to do with maturity and experience—or at least the perception of having them.

"In the start-up world, *failure* is almost synonymous with *learning experience,"* she says. "Being a founder who has failed before signals to the community that, one, you've done this before, and, two, you've gathered information on what doesn't work and are better armed to create something that does."

All good reasons not to let failure hold you back. In fact, it might just make you more successful than you ever dreamed.

---

7 Failures That Helped Richard Branson Become a Multi-billionaire

Since Richard Branson opened his first Virgin Records store in 1972, his Virgin Group has tried to enter a number of spaces, from makeup to vodka. But not every new venture has been a success. Here's what Branson says he learned from seven of his biggest failures.

1. ***Student* magazine.** Branson's first venture was a magazine run by students. He envisioned the Student brand would eventually include travel companies and banks. When a potential acquisition failed, it was for the best— the acquirer didn't share Branson's big vision.

2. **Virgin Records' legal trouble.** In 1971, Branson sold discs at Virgin Records that were designated for export—thus avoiding a 33 percent tax. After getting caught, Branson was slapped with a £60,000 fine. After the incident, Branson knew he needed to get more serious about the business.

3. Virgin Cola. Branson tried to put Coca-Cola out of business with the launch of Virgin Cola in 1994. But business fizzled by 2012, and Branson said Virgin made the mistake of not offering something "radically different enough" from Coca-Cola.

4. Virgin Cars. From 2000 to 2005, the Virgin Group had a little-known site where people could buy and sell cars. Branson said he thought Virgin Cars failed because he had the "wrong angle," and he should have explored an auto business centered around sustainability.

5. VirginStudent.com. A precursor to Facebook and My-Space, VirginStudent, launched in 2000, didn't gain traction quickly enough, and was shut down in 2005. In a blog post, Branson said the venture did open his eyes to how powerful social media would become one day.

6. Virgin Pulse. Virgin knew that it had to come up with a competing product as Apple's iPod started to take off in 2004. But by the time Virgin Pulse was out, it was already too late. Branson said the experience taught the team not to be afraid to exit markets too early.

7. Virgin Brides. Branson publicized the 1996 launch of Virgin's bridal store by dressing up as a bride. By 2005, Virgin Brides was no more. Branson mused that it failed because "there aren't many virgin brides," or because promotional pictures of him in a dress (Google it) were a turn-off.

WHAT TO DO IF YOU'RE UNCERTAIN...
OR MAYBE EVEN STUCK?

You may say you don't have an idea, let alone a vision. If this is the case, then consider the advice of bestselling business book author Paul B. Brown.

"The reality is when you dig a little deeper, invariably you find you have *lots* of ideas—'Maybe I'll open a restaurant; maybe a personal shopper service,'" Brown says. In fact, you might have a whole notebook full of ideas—none of which you have pursued. So why did nothing happen?

Maybe you thought none of them were any good. Or maybe you spent all your time trying to refine them, or playing "what if" games, pondering dozens or hundreds of scenarios that might or might not happen.

"In this kind of situation, you would be far better off getting out and doing something, because action changes reality and thinking doesn't," Brown says.

When you take action, you understand a little bit more about what you're trying to create. You gain more knowledge. You learn about opportunities, whether that's potential partners or even more innovative avenues to follow. By contrast, when you sit alone at your desk just thinking and not acting, nothing happens.

Sure, ideas can arise in a flash of insight. But more often (and more reliably) your ultimate idea will surface and develop through your interactions with other people or the marketplace. You don't need the idea as much as you need to get started. Worst case? You take a few tiny steps and discover you don't like what you're doing.

Or maybe you decide it's impossible. If that happens, you reboot and move onto something else.

● ● ●

In this chapter, we've taken an in-depth look at the first stage of your entrepreneurial journey—how to come up with your remarkable, brilliant, kick-ass idea. In the pages ahead, we'll take a look at the next steps, outlining the typical approaches that entrepreneurs take to get their startup ideas off the ground. We'll also dive into the practicalities, from choosing a legal structure for your business to obtaining permits and licenses.

SELECT THE BEST STRATEGY AND STRUCTURE FOR YOUR STARTUP

> " When you walk into a room, if you don't know more about your industry, your customer, your business than anyone else in the world...someone like me is going to come in and kick your ass."

—

MARK CUBAN, serial entrepreneur, owner of the NBA's Dallas Mavericks and shark on ABC's *Shark Tank*.

AS YOU'VE PROBABLY GLEANED BY now, entrepreneurship requires far more than just a brilliant business idea. (If that were the case, this book would have been a lot shorter.) Now that you've worked out a concept, it's time for the tricky part: figuring out how to turn your vision into reality.

It's our opinion at *Inc.* that the next step of the entrepreneurial journey is the business plan—or at the very least, a rough version of what will *become* your formal business plan. Whether you're a mom-and-pop bakery or an up-and-coming tech company, it's wise to get your startup idea out of your head and onto paper (or an online document).

What's a business plan, exactly? Simply put, it is a living, breathing document that describes your concept, outlines your goals, and maps out the strategies you'll take (whether that's marketing to customers or raising money from investors) to turn your idea into a successful company.

> **❝** Entrepreneurs are people who dream up new ideas, and then commercialize them into new businesses. Most people believe that the hard part is coming up with the idea, and the easy part is turning it into a business. Yet, in my experience as a mentor to entrepreneurs, the majority of failures I see are related to starting and growing the business, not developing the solution."

MARTIN ZWILLING, veteran startup mentor and founder of Startup Professionals

Now, right away, we want to be clear. When the topic of business plans comes up, it tends to polarize people into two separate camps:

1. Those who think business plans are worth the effort to put together

2. Those who think writing business plans is a waste of time (except, perhaps, if you're trying to raise money)

So, who's right? We spoke to Ellen Rohr, founder of Bare Bones Biz, a venture capital and consulting company, who says the answer lies somewhere in between.

"The *primary* purpose of a business plan is to help you gain clarity and hold yourself accountable for moving in the direction of what you want," she says. (For more on the benefits of that, please see "Five Reasons Why You Need a Business Plan," page 49.) "The *secondary* purpose is to attract investors, or get a loan, or get buy-in from your spouse, partner, parent, kid, team members, or whomever," she says. "Unless you have your intentions for your business written down, you might miss an opportunity to communicate it to someone else or even to clarify things for yourself."

Are business plans ever a complete waste of time? Possibly, if writing a full-blown business plan takes weeks or months of your effort, or distracts you from getting going, which is a big reason why that second camp tends to discount them. (Please see "The Case Against Writing a Business Plan," page 59.)

In recent years, much emphasis has been placed on the "lean startup" method, popularized by Eric Ries and Steve Blank, in which an entrepreneur essentially starts the process of developing a company in real time. (More on that later in the chapter.) We're fans of the lean startup method, in which an entrepreneur typically puts a bare-bones version on the market, getting customer feedback and making constant iterations to the business model. The method de-emphasizes the old-school business plan, instead emphasizing "think big, start small, fail quickly, scale fast."

Anecdotally, we find most successful entrepreneurs tend to land somewhere in the middle. They incorporate bits and pieces of both schools of thought, starting out with a simple business idea, testing it, tweaking it, and sometimes pivoting wildly if customer feedback demands it. (Please see case study of Slack on page 68.) Then they eventually encapsulate product descriptions, market strategies, and sales goals into a formal business plan as the company takes shape or as the need arises. And usually, that "need" is financing—most lenders will want to see a business plan, and most investors will want to see at minimum the executive summary of a business plan.

In the earliest stages, we recommend crafting at least an informal business plan (see page 58) in which you highlight key elements that define your vision while outlining initial activities or milestones that will drive you toward your goal.

> ❝ Build sports car. Use that money to build an affordable car. Use that money to build an even more affordable car. While doing above, also provide zero emission electric power generation options. Don't tell anyone."
>
> —
> **ELON MUSK,** summarizing his business plan in 2006 in a blog post on Tesla's website

In the pages ahead, we'll take a look at the formal business plan—which (at the least) should get you thinking about the nitty-gritty of your startup, including mission, business model, structure, existing strategic relationships, and your ultimate plan for profitability.

Will having a business plan make success inevitable? Absolutely not. But great planning often means the difference between success and failure.

Five Reasons Why You Need a Business Plan

Starting a business? You should write a business plan—even if you're not raising money anytime soon, says *Inc.* columnist David Ronick, a serial entrepreneur. Here's why Ronick thinks they are a must.

1. **It will help you avoid big mistakes.** The last thing you want to do is work on your startup for a year, only to realize you were doomed to fail from the start. Many founders learn the hard way that they underestimated capital needs or took on partners with the wrong skills or lacked a viable way to make money. Developing a business plan can help ensure that you're sprinting down the right path.

2. **It will help counterbalance emotions.** During the start-up phase, you're prone to be "manic"—so passionate about your ideas that you lose sight of reality. At other times, you'll be overwhelmed by doubt, fear, or exhaustion. When emotions peak, a business plan helps you step back and take an objective look at what you are doing and why.

3. **It will make sure everyone's on the same page.** Chances are, you are not building a company by yourself. Ideally, you'll have partners, so you can launch faster, smarter, and with less need to pay employees or suppli-

ers. Even if you don't have partners, you'll have family, friends, and advisors involved. Sharing your business plan keeps everyone headed in the same direction.

4. **It will help you develop a game plan.** At a startup, execution is everything. That means you have to set priorities, establish goals, and measure performance. You also need to identify the key questions to answer, like "What features do customers really want?" "Will customers buy our product and how much will they pay?" and "How can we attract customers in a way that's cost effective and scalable?" These are all things you'll address during the business planning process.

5. **It will help you raise capital.** If you raise or borrow money—even from friends and family—you'll need to communicate your vision in a clear, compelling way. A good business plan will help you do just that. A study by Babson College found that startups with a business plan raised twice as much capital as those without a business plan within the first twelve months.

HOW TO WRITE A BUSINESS PLAN

A classic business plan is a blueprint for your business that can help you navigate and manage your company while also helping potential investors, partners, lenders, and others understand your business strategy and your chances at success.

A business plan, typically thirty pages or so in length, is never quite finished because you're ideally always revising it, reviewing it, and building upon it. In fact, more critical to your business's future than a plan is the process "that you undertake on a regular basis to hopefully keep your ship headed in the right direction without losing sight of your long-term destination," says long-time business journalist Elizabeth Wasserman, who has written extensively on the issue.

If you're just starting out, writing a business plan can help you describe your product or service, detail your marketing strategy, and lay out your sales and operational forecasts—including the ever-important cash-flow projection so as to keep your business on track for profits.

If you're seeking investment or loans, whether from venture capitalists or bankers or others, a business plan (at the very least, the executive summary) is often essential. It's one of the first documents that a loan officer will want to see. In addition, an angel or venture capital investor will want to see not only the executive summary before providing funding, but they'll try to poke holes in your plan and quiz you about things you should have addressed. For the purpose of financing, you may add certain sections to your business plan, including background and historical information about the business and a description of the management team leading the organization.

If you're developing a plan involving a business loan, then your lenders are going to want something slightly different. They will want to see a section detailing collateral, or assets to pledge against the loan. Collateral includes funds to support loan payments, interest expenses, and debt repayment. Banks won't make speculative loans, so you need to include information in your plan to make the banker feel safe.

If you need help, consult the Small Business Administration's on-line guide to business plans (www.sba.gov) or peruse over a hundred free sample business plans at Palo Alto Software's Bplans.com.

❝❝ I actually wrote a 75-page business plan for Learnvest. Please do not do that. No one asked for it, no one read it. But what was important about it: It was for me. If any other person ever challenged me, I knew the answers. And what I mean by that: What's the problem, what's the market, who's the customer. I knew who the competitors were. So, when I was jumping off the cliff, I wasn't saying, "Oh, I'll figure it out on the way down." Once you get up and you're running a business, your hair's on fire. You're putting out X, Y, Z problem. You're not in a position to say, "What's my strategy." Now, I'm leading 115 people. If I didn't have a clear strategy, I don't know if everyone would get out of bed in the morning, excited to come work for me."

—
ALEXA VON TOBEL, founder of Learnvest, a personal finance website

Killer Business Plans

There are plenty of websites out there that offer to sell business plan templates for $20 or more, designed to let you enter your company name and specifics and generate a plan.

While that may be tempting, a generic business plan sample with your details just dumped in isn't going to wow anyone, and it's not going to inspire you on a regular basis, says Larry Kim, founder of WordStream, an online marketing company.

"I know from experience that the last thing you have when you're starting your own business is an abundance of time to dream up creative ideas for your business plan," Kim says. "Don't worry—you don't have to reinvent the wheel."

He recommends using the following business plan templates, many of the "less is more" variety:

1. **Business Plan Infographic PowerPoint, available on GraphicRiver.net.** Present your market analysis, timeline, statistics, and more in an engaging and highly visual infographic.

2. **Lean Canvas 1-Page Business Plan, Leanstack.com.** You can create a one-page business model in a speedy twenty minutes.

3. **Startup X—Perfect Pitch Deck PowerPoint Template, GraphicRiver.net.** This one stands out in a sea of PowerPoint business plan templates, thanks to the creative modifications you can make.

4. **Emaze Business Plan With Analytics, Emaze.com.** More than just a template, this comprehensive presentation tool features collaboration and analytics.

5. **Startup Pitch, GraphicRiver.net.** This PowerPoint-format business plan sample has a creative tear-away design that's eye catching and unique.

6. **Palo Alto Software's LivePlan, LivePlan.com.** This is another easy-to-use tool where you input your information and it creates a one-page, infographic-style business plan for you.

COMPONENTS OF A BUSINESS PLAN

Most formal business plans contain the following components, although the order in which you write and present these sections is subject to change:

→ **Executive Summary.** This is the abstract of your business plan, a summary of everything you will say in greater detail in the ensuing pages. It spells out the content and goals of your plan, hitting all the highlights. This section is key if you are seeking outside funding, as it introduces possible investors to your business. Be sure to include background about your company, the market opportunity, your capital requirements, a mission statement, an overview of management, competitors, your business's competitive advantages, and a summary of your financial projections over the next three years. "Some people write the executive summary first, but I would never do that," says Linda Pinson, author of *Anatomy of a Business Plan*. "I would go through and write my plan first and come back to the executive summary." Keep this to no more than three or four pages.

→ **Company Overview.** The company overview is designed to provide more information about your business, why and when it was formed, its mission, business model, strategy, and any existing strategic relationships. Pinson recommends including administrative issues, such as intellectual property you may own, costs associated with your location, the legal structure of your company, management, personnel, and how you address accounting, legal, insurance, and security matters.

→ **Business Offering.** Here's where you talk about why you're in business and what you're selling, whether it's products and/or services. If you sell products, state whether you are the manufacturer, distributor, and/or retailer of a product and talk about your manufacturing process, availability of materials, how you handle inventory and fulfillment, etc. If you provide services, describe those services. Make sure to address any new product lines or service lines that you expect to enter into in the future.

→ **Marketing Plan and Analysis.** In this section, you spell out your marketing strategy (see more on that in Chapter 4), addressing details of your market analysis, sales, customer service, advertising, and public relations. Many businesses use this space to showcase their vision of why their business will be successful, backing that up with market research that identifies their target market and industry and customer trends. But most of the time, small and mid-sized businesses don't have the deep pockets to hire outside firms to undertake exhaustive market research. "A sizeable majority of smaller entrepreneurial companies are going to bet the company on their own sense of the market without the validation of outside research," says Tim Berry, chairman and founder of Palo Alto Software, maker of Business Plan Pro software. In lieu of research, Berry, who is also an investor, says companies can provide testimonials from existing customers.

→ **Strategy and Implementation.** Every business plan needs details. This section is where many should go. "This is where I'm going to be looking as an investor for dates and deadlines," Berry says. "I'll be looking for things we'll be able to track," whether that's product release dates or unique visitors. This is also a section in which to include your sales forecasts, Berry says.

→ **Management Team.** If writing the business plan for investors or bankers, you want to explain the background of your company executives and managers and explain how that will help you meet business goals. "For investors, it's an important element to include who these people are and what their experience is," Berry says. "Investors need to evaluate risk, and the general assumption is that management team experience greatly affects risk. The more seasoned the management team, the less the risk." If writing this solely for internal purposes, you may want to explain how managers expect to grow the staff of the business in the future to meet business objectives.

→ **Financial Projections.** In the financial section, you provide "the quantitative interpretation" of everything you stated in your organizational and marketing sections, Pinson says. She also advises not to write the financial section until those other sections are complete. This is where you include your projected profit and loss statements, your balance sheet, and your cash flow statements for the next three years. "Those are forward-looking projections," Berry points out. "It's not your accounting." That's often a source of confusion. The order of the numbers will be very much like they appear in accounting statements but they will be forecasts for the future. "Accounting is today backward into the past," Berry says. "Planning is today forward into the future.'

You may want to include supporting documents to back up statements or decisions you've made. These should be included in a separate section. These supplemental materials might include resumes of your managers, credit reports, copies of leases or contracts, or letters of reference from people who can attest that you are a reputable and reliable businessperson.

The business plan, according to Berry, is far more than just a document. It's actually "the content, the strategy, and the specifics of what is going to happen to your business," he says.

HOW TO WRITE AN INFORMAL BUSINESS PLAN

If you're not seeking investors, or want to jump into the market quickly to launch your product or service, then an *informal* business plan can help you clarify your startup's goals, sales strategy, and target market. At the least, writing it all down will help you crystallize your thoughts, set your priorities, and keep you on track.

An informal business plan should contain, at the minimum:

A company description and mission statement. Describe your business in a few brief paragraphs, including your legal structure (for more on that, see pages 70–75) and the type of unique services or products you provide. Also include a brief description of the management team, detailing each person's responsibilities.

An overview of your target market. Be specific about the customers you serve, including any demographics you might have, such as age, income, location, purchasing habits, buying cycles, and willingness to adopt new products and services. A goal in this section is to prove that you know your customer, which is important for marketing your company.

An overview of the competition. Identify the current (or potential) competitors in your area or online who sell a service or product similar to yours, and identify their strengths and weaknesses. Gather this information by checking out their websites and marketing materials, or visiting their locations.

Marketing and sales strategy. Describe how you will promote your business, whether that's through advertising, social media campaigns, promotional literature, or public relations. Define how you will get your product or service to customers, including whether you need sales representatives (inside or external) to promote your products. Identify what differentiates you, particularly when it comes to price, product, or service.

An overview of your finances. Include your startup costs, your operating costs, and revenue estimates. Keep your expectations realistic and honest: The biggest mistake entrepreneurs can make is to be overly optimistic with sales estimates. Include a cash-flow statement, as lack of cash is one of the biggest reasons small businesses fail.

THE CASE AGAINST WRITING A BUSINESS PLAN

A formal business plan is a waste of your time—and that's true even if you plan to raise money from investors, says *Inc.* columnist Geoffrey James.

The conventional wisdom, James explains, is that investors *require* a three- to five-year business plan, since they'll look for their investment return in that time frame. But there's scant evidence that's the case, he says. Here's why.

"First off, for a startup, three years is the distant future and five years might as well be in another geological epoch," he says. "It's ludicrous to pretend you have any idea what you or your firm will be doing in five years.'

Second, he says, nobody has time to read a formal document, especially one that follows the typical template that wastes pages on irrelevancies like corporate mission, personal background, and pie-in-the-sky projections.

"Finally, the fact that you wasted—what, maybe an entire week?—writing a formal document that nobody (including you) wants to read is a certain signal to savvy investors that you lack a sense of priority," he says.

Rather than a formal business plan, some investors prefer a ten-slide presentation (also known as a "pitch deck") built around a demo or prototype, he says. Simplify your ideas so you can describe them on a single written page.

Remember, even the corporate world simultaneously uses and dismisses three- and five-year plans. "It's been that way for decades," James says. "So, no, you don't need a formal business plan to get your startup off the ground. And you don't need to spend precious hours polishing and updating it."

That time is better spent doing something useful, he says...such as making your idea work in the real world.

A LOOK AT THE LEAN STARTUP METHOD

In 2011, entrepreneur Eric Ries published a book called *The Lean Startup*, describing a startup methodology designed to eliminate waste that focuses on building a minimum viable product or MVP. It quickly became dogma in Silicon Valley.

Ries's lean principles, which focus on rapid iteration rather than long development cycles, have since been embraced by old-school companies (think General Electric) and recommended for just about anyone starting a business. At its core, the lean startup method is a disciplined process, one that embraces experimentation, rapid proto-typing, and constant learning from customer feedback.

> **"** Now that I have my own startup, I've not only gotten the Lean Startup religion; I've become downright evangelical. We implement lean processes in just about everything we do, and we have from the start."
>
> —
> **THOMAS GOETZ,** CEO and co-founder, Iodine

In a question-and-answer session with *Inc.*, Ries explained his thinking behind the methodology and provided his best tips on how entrepreneurs can apply it.

Q *You've started several companies that subsequently folded. What's the biggest mistake that startups make?*

Startups make so many mistakes that the challenge to identify the root cause of a failure is tough. But believing in your own plan is probably the worst. In our case, we were convinced that if we did a really good job developing and implementing a good plan (writing a business plan, doing focus groups—all the traditional stuff), we would be rewarded with success. If I showed you the business plans, they were incredibly well-written. The only problem is that reality didn't conform to our plan. We didn't bother to double-check our plan—we just assumed we were correct and that's where most of us go wrong.

So, from this idea, you formed the concept of the "Lean Startup." How can entrepreneurs actually employ your strategy?

The fundamental idea is to treat everything a startup does as an experiment. Everything a startup does should be a test—a hypothesis. You really want to organize your company so that it's built to learn. *The Lean Startup* idea is based on lean manufacturing—a management philosophy that we can easily adapt to the startup culture. A key part is creating a feedback loop: build, measure, and learn. We want to get through that loop as quickly as possible. But it's not just failing fast, it's failing well.

A big part of your theory is to engage the customers early on and to test things. How do you find customers if you don't have a final product or a well-known brand?

Testing with only friends and family is a bad idea. Friends and family are more likely to give you positive feedback—and that's not helpful. But this part should be easy for entrepreneurs. One of the assumptions you've probably built into your business plan is how you will get customers after the product is done. You can follow that plan right now to get started on finding those customers. Most entrepreneurs don't need as many customers as they think. A lot of people think ten is too few for a sample. But if all ten refused a product, why is that not enough? If you want a hundred, a thousand, or a million customers, you first have to get ten. But the answer for every business is different. It will be a different size if you're selling a B2B product versus a product for teenagers.

How do you test your concept without finalizing the product you plan to take to market?

What you want to do is create the "minimum viable product." That's essentially the smallest, simplest version of your product that allows you to begin that process of learning. What I mean by "minimal" is not just referring to features on a product, but also minimal in the number of people to show it to. The most common way to do it is to allow people to pre-order a product [doesn't have to be online] before it's ready. If your campaign fails, you never have to build the product. You can do this with almost any business.

Q *Can you give an example?*

A Zappos. I often ask people how they would build Zappos. You need a good selection and customer service option, they'll say. You'd need to build a big call center, a big distribution center, etc. But the MVP for them was as follows: They went to a local shoe store, took pictures of each of their products, and put them online. If anyone bought shoes from them [at this early stage], they planned to go to the store, buy the shoes and mail them to the customer. There was no big business behind it; there was a website and a hope that they'll get so many orders that it will get annoying to do all the purchasing and shipping manually. It was all to test their big idea.

Q *Sometimes entrepreneurs learn that their product is all wrong, but you think that's not a horrible thing. It can lead to what you call a "pivot" in your business plan.*

A You don't need to fail before you pivot. A pivot is simply a change in strategy without a change in vision. Whenever entrepreneurs see a new way to achieve their vision—a way to be more successful—they have to remain nimble enough to take it.

AND NOW THE PRACTICAL:
PERMITS AND PAPERWORK

The administrative process of starting your own company is surprisingly simple. In fact, Inc.com columnist Jeff Haden estimates that aspiring entrepreneurs can clear all the hurdles in under three hours.

"Keep in mind, I'm only talking about setting yourself up to do business—I'm not talking about writing a business plan, sourcing financing, developing a marketing plan, etc.," Haden says. "The goal is to get off square one and get on to the fun stuff."

Here's a checklist:

1. **Pick a name so you can get the administrative ball rolling.** While a business name is important, don't needlessly agonize over the process—especially if it delays you from starting up. Remember, your business can operate under a different name than your company name. (A "doing business as" form takes minutes to complete.) And you can change your company name later, if you like.

2. **Get your Employer Identification Number.** An EIN is the federal tax number used to identify your business. Technically, you only need an EIN if you will have employees or plan to form a partnership, LLC, or corporation. But even if you don't need an EIN, get one anyway: It's free, takes minutes, and you can keep your Social Security number private, thereby reducing the chance of identity theft. (When you don't have an EIN, you must use your SSN to

identify your business for tax purposes.) Apply online for an EIN at www.irs.gov.

3. **Obtain a business license.** For this, head to your locality's administrative office (or website). Most counties or cities require a business license, typically for tax purposes but sometimes—depending on your industry—to protect public health and safety. The form is easy and quick to fill out. Use your EIN instead of your Social Security number to identify your business. If asked for annual gross receipts, do your best to estimate accurately.

4. **Ask your locality about other permits or paperwork.** "In my area, for example, a home occupation permit is required to verify that a business based in a home meets zoning requirements," Haden says. "Your locality may require other permits. Ask. They'll tell you." Some cities or towns may require that you register a trade name (in most cases, you'll get approved on the spot) or complete a business personal-property tax form.

5. **Get a certificate of resale (if necessary).** A certificate of resale, also known as a seller's permit, allows you to collect state sales tax on products sold. (In some states, there is also a sales tax on services like cleaning or repair.) You will need a seller's permit if you plan to sell products. Your state department of taxation's website can provide online forms, or most localities have forms you can complete while you're at their administrative offices.

6. **Get a business bank account.** One of the easiest ways to screw up your business accounting and possibly run afoul of the IRS is to commingle personal and business funds (and transactions). Using a business account helps eliminate that possibility. Get a business account using your business name and EIN, and only use that account for all business-related deposits, withdrawals, and transactions. Pick a bank or local credit union that is convenient.

7. **Set up a simple accounting spreadsheet.** Worry about business accounting software like QuickBooks later. For now, just create a spreadsheet on which you can enter money you spend and money you receive. Bookkeeping is simple, at least at first. All you need are Revenue and Expenses columns; you can add line items as you go. As long as you record everything you do now, creating a more formal system later will be fairly easy.

"And now you're an entrepreneur, with all the documents to prove it," Haden says.

Slack, an Example of Pivoting and Planning

SLACK, THE GROUP-MESSAGING system, is one of the fastest-growing business applications in the world. But it didn't start life as the workplace productivity tool that millions of people now use.

In 2009, entrepreneur Stewart Butterfield, who had previously co-founded photo-sharing website Flickr, decided to launch a social gaming company in Vancouver. The startup, called Tiny Speck, quickly raised $1.5 million in early-stage financing. While it spent four years as a gaming company, its main product—a game called *Glitch*—couldn't sustain the business.

In October 2012, Butterfield and his partners made the decision to shut down *Glitch* (he recalls breaking down in tears, telling his forty-person staff). They offered investors their remaining money back, about $5 million, but were told to keep it and try to build something else with a skeleton crew.

They hit on one idea so obvious no one remembers exactly who suggested it first. While building Glitch, the team had been communicating via an internal communication system. It was a messaging tool "which we really liked," Butterfield says. Maybe other companies would like it too? "It was a very short hop from there to "we should try to make this a product."

Over the next seventeen days, Butterfield typed out a pitch deck (a presentation, usually based on slides, that provides investors with an overview of your business). He outlined what Slack would be: All your team communication in one place, instantly searchable, available wherever you go, a platform that "builds up to the edge" of other applications, like Excel or PowerPoint, but doesn't seek to reproduce them. Almost to a letter, it's the roadmap Slack has followed.

Some 8,000 companies signed up for Slack as soon as it launched. Within a year, it had 140,000 daily users. In October 2014, Slack officially became a unicorn (a tech startup worth more than $1 billion). By January 2017, it had more than 5 million daily users and had raised $540 million in funding.

An investor in Slack, Twitter co-founder Biz Stone, says aspiring entrepreneurs can learn from the company's story. "Build a prototype just to see if your idea is a thing or not," says Stone, who had invested in Slack when it still was a game developer. "You have to start somewhere and see where it takes you." And then once you've found your way, map out the rest of the journey to success.

—

NEXT STEPS:
PICKING A LEGAL STRUCTURE

Legally speaking, it's easy to start a company.

By default—meaning, if you do absolutely nothing—your startup is a sole proprietorship or partnership, unless you and your co-founders (if any) opt for another structure. Such a business is not distinct from its owners, and its income is reported on your personal income tax returns.

And therein lies the key drawback of a sole proprietorship or partnership: You have unlimited liability for your business's debts. You are personally liable for deals your partners make, even if you have an agreement that limits individual authority. And a mistake can cost you not just the company but everything you own.

So, if you are starting a business, or if you already run one but haven't thought strategically about its legal structure, you need to take this matter seriously. For limited liability protection—limited, that is, to what you have invested in your company—the choices come down to a limited liability company or a corporation. The decision is more complicated than it may seem: What the government leaves in one pocket, it takes from another. So, sit down with a lawyer and accountant to weigh the options in light of your individual tax situation.

Keep in mind that liability protections are not absolute. Creditors may be able to pierce the corporate veil that separates a company from its owners' personal assets in cases of fraud, when the entities are inextricably linked, or when the company fails to adhere to the basic legal and reporting requirements.

When comparing options (LLC versus corporations), the principal decision is whether you want your company to pay taxes on profits before they are distributed to owners or you want the profits to flow straight through to the owners' individual tax returns.

Remember, you have a certain amount of flexibility when it comes to changing the legal structure of your business and you can easily convert from an S corp to a C corp.

Here's what you need to know:

Limited Liability Company

This structure essentially melds a partnership with the limited liability protection offered by a corporation. The LLC is a fairly recent innovation—most states didn't recognize it until the mid-1990s—but because of its flexibility, lawyers have come to recommend it for most small companies. Depending on the state, the owners of an LLC (called members) can consist of a single individual, two or more individuals, corporations, partnerships, trusts, or other LLCs.

How it works: Like a partnership, an LLC is a pass-through entity, meaning that profits, losses, credits, and deductions flow through to your personal tax returns. An owner can use losses to offset other income, but only up to the amount he or she invested, which is called the basis. In an LLC, unlike a corporation, income and losses can be distributed unequally among members—the LLC could, for example, allow one member to take all of the losses but allocate profits based on ownership interest.

Watch out for: LLC members can't distinguish between income earned as salary and passive investment income, so profits are subject to Social Security and Medicare taxes on top of income taxes.

How to file an LLC: After choosing a unique name (which must end in a variation of Limited Liability Company), you file articles of organization with your state. Many states allow you to do so online; others provide a template to use. Though not required by law, an operating agreement that defines the basic rights and responsibilities of the LLC's members is also crucial. New York requires notice of the LLC's formation to be published, which adds to startup costs.

C corporation

This is the basic type of American corporation—a legal entity that's completely separate from its owners. Because its shares can be traded among an unlimited number and types of owners, the C corp is the vehicle commonly used for taking a company public. Generally speaking, entrepreneurs choose the C corp structure if they hope to attract professional investors or reward employees with stock. Many small businesses prefer other structures, to avoid the C corp's "double taxation" (more on that below) and requirements to hold board and shareholder meetings.

How it works: The corporation files its own tax return and pays taxes on its income at the corporate rate. When profits are distributed to shareholders in the form of dividends, they are taxed again—a double tax, some argue—at shareholders' individual income tax rates. However, because the corporate tax rate tends to be lower than the individual tax rate, some experts recommend a C corp for small companies that reinvest profits. Unlike an LLC, a C corp can distinguish between active and passive income and pay employment taxes only on the salaries of the active shareholders.

S corporation

The S corp has long reigned as the way to avoid the C corp's double taxation. Ownership in an S corp is restricted to no more than 100 U.S. shareholders (a family can count as a single shareholder), with one class of stock. Normally, an S corp cannot be owned by another company or own one. Still, it remains a good choice for companies that can't legally organize as LLCs (such as banks or insurers) or would face higher taxes as LLCs, which is the case in some states.

How it works: In S corps, income flows through to the individual shareholders, and federal tax is paid at the owner level. (Most states follow suit, but a few tax S corps at the company level in certain cases. Also, New York City doesn't recognize S corps and taxes them as C corps.) Owners of S corps can enjoy tax savings by paying themselves "reasonable" salaries tied to industry norms, subject to self-employment taxes, and then take a distribution of profits, which is free of employment taxes.

How to incorporate: Incorporation begins by selecting a name and filing articles of incorporation, which in most states simply entails completing a registration form. (Filing fees vary by state, from $100 to $1,000.) Then, the founders must appoint directors and draft the company's bylaws, which stipulate how the business will operate. Finally, the new corporation must deliver stock certificates to its shareholders.

If you need help, more information and legal forms are available online at Nolo.com and LegalZoom.com.

Becoming a Certified B Corp or Benefit Corporation

Attention social entrepreneurs: You can structure your business so that "doing good" is part of your for-profit business model.

By becoming a certified B corp and/or benefit corporation (which are similar but different), you can factor in non-financial goals—say, saving the environment—along with the bottom line when you're making decisions for your company.

The B corp designation was popularized by B Lab, a Berwyn, Pennsylvania, nonprofit founded in 2006. B Lab will certify a company in any of the fifty states as a "B corp" after it's met rigorous standards of social and environmental performance, accountability, and transparency. The label is akin to other certifications, such as Leadership in Energy and Environmental

Design (LEED) or Fair Trade. Well-known B corps include Patagonia, Ben & Jerry's, and Warby Parker.

As part of the certification process, B Lab requires companies in most states to eventually become a benefit corporation (a legal designation similar to C corp). As of July 2017, thirty-three states and the District of Columbia have allowed this new type of corporation. The status essentially provides a company with greater freedom to pursue social goals without fear of being sued by shareholders for failing to maximize profits.

If you want more information, the Yale Center for Business and the Environment and Patagonia have published *An Entrepreneur's Guide to Certified B Corporations and Benefit Corporations*, available for download at cbey.yale.edu.

We've outlined some of the early choices you'll need to make as you turn your idea into a company. In the next chapter, we'll answer your most pressing questions about money, the lifeblood of any young business.

FIGURE OUT FUNDING

" 'Fundraising is going to be the death of me!' That's how I've felt, oh, perhaps ten times throughout my journey to date as a serial entrepreneur."

—

DAVE KERPEN, founder and CEO of Likeable Local, a social media software company.

IT'S ALWAYS DAUNTING TO RAISE money for a startup. Most entrepreneurs are forced to dive into their own pockets for the cash to start a business, as few lenders or investors want to bet on an unproven startup. Newbie entrepreneurs often cobble together funds by combining their own savings with a few other sources (such as loved ones, credit cards, or home-equity loans) in the early months or years. Those who don't have enough cash sometimes try crowdfunding sites. It remains difficult or downright impossible for startups to obtain bank loans. That's because banks and credit unions are risk-averse and don't want to take a chance on a startup until much later, when the business has a track record and financial statements to prove it.

A small number of startups, often in the technology realm, will try to raise money from investors. This route is only appropriate for businesses that have exit strategies (in other words, they plan to one day go public or sell themselves to a larger company, which is when investors reap profits). If that's you, starting your capital search with a good business plan will show investors your company's potential.

Finding and securing startup cash can take careful research, good negotiation skills, and, above all, an unflagging commitment to your new business. Here's a look at the most common sources of funding for small businesses.

SOURCE:
YOU

Far and away, the most common source of startup funding is you—meaning your savings, credit cards, retirement savings, or home equity loans. We'll take a look at each below. Some good news: Entrepreneurs who have started this way—and most have—say having "skin in the game" can teach early lessons in frugality and impresses lenders or investors down the road.

> **"** I started Learnvest out of my savings account. I started paying designers, paying technologists tiny chunks of checks. Because I was actually paying for things myself with my own savings, it sharpened my focus of how to spend money. Quickly you'll be able to say, we don't need that."
>
> **ALEXA VON TOBEL,** founder of personal-finance website Learnvest, which ultimately raised $69 million in venture capital and was acquired by Northwestern Mutual for a reported $250 million

Your bank account

No matter if the economy is soaring or tanking, this is where you start. Exactly how much you need depends on your business (please see "Calculating Startup Costs," page 83). And exactly how much you want to risk may depend on your circumstances in life: Are you single? Married with college-bound children? Getting ready to retire? All of this requires some soul searching and (in some cases) discussion with significant others in your life.

Now, a key to investing in your own business is not to put every last penny of your savings into your new, unproven startup. Personal-finance experts recommend keeping enough in an emergency savings account to cover at least three months of personal expenses (like the mortgage, groceries, and utilities). If you're a newly minted business owner—meaning, you're not yet drawing a salary—you'll likely need considerably more, especially if sales take longer than expected to come in. You'll want to keep extra cash in a reserve, in the event unplanned business expenses arise in your startup's early years.

Credit cards

Many entrepreneurs use personal credit cards to fund their startups, which can be risky. Fall behind on your payment and your credit score gets whacked. Pay just the minimum each month and you could create a hole you'll never get out of. That said, if used responsibly, a credit card can get you out of the occasional jam and even extend your accounts payable period to shore up your cash flow. Note: most startups aren't eligible for business lines of credit until they are more established. Once you have a line of credit, though, you can use it as a short-term bridge loan to cover working capital needs.

Home equity loans

If you're a homeowner, you might consider tapping into home equity to fund a business. In that case, you might consider a home equity loan, which, like a mortgage, usually has a fixed rate and monthly payment. Or you could look into a home equity line of credit or HELOC, which functions more like a credit card, with a variable interest rate. But here's the thing: If your brilliant idea turns out to be less-than-brilliant, you still have to repay the loan or lose your house. Some experts recommend saving home equity funds as a source of capital for down the road, for when your revenue-generating business has reliable customers.

Retirement savings

One of the worst ideas is to dip into retirement savings to fund your startup—although plenty of entrepreneurs do it. If you've left a corporate job (or are thinking about it), those funds you've accumulated in your 401(k) over the years can look pretty tempting. Technically, if you set up a C corporation and roll your retirement assets into it, you can tap them without penalty. If you're considering this, make sure to talk with an accountant, as the steps are legally complex. But remember: If things don't pan out, not only do you lose your business, but your nest egg, too.

❝ I probably had about twenty grand in the bank when Under Armour started. A lot of money for a college kid. I ended up going to just under $40,000 in credit card debt spread across five cards. In the summer of 1997, I was totally broke—so broke I needed to go to my mom's house to ask if she minded cooking dinner for me. I needed for her to feed me. Then all of a sudden I started getting my first round of orders."

—

KEVIN PLANK, founder of athletic-apparel business Under Armour, now a $5 billion public company

---

Calculating Startup Costs

How much money do you need to start a business?

The answer, of course, is unique to your startup, which will have its own specific cash needs at various stages in its developmental cycle. For example, a service-based business with no inventory (think Uber, a transportation company that doesn't actually own any vehicles) can be started on a small budget. Other startups—a restaurant, for example—will need to invest a substantial amount in inventory or equipment.

While there's no universal method for estimating startup costs, the Small Business Administration provides a few helpful tips at its website, www.sba.gov.

First, figure out how much seed money you'll need by estimating the costs of being in business for the first months. "Some of these expenses will be one-time costs such as the fee for incorporating your business or the price of a sign for your building," according to the SBA. "Some will be ongoing costs, such as the cost of utilities, inventory, insurance, etc."

When you're analyzing those costs, decide which are essential and which are optional. "A realistic startup budget should only include those things that are necessary to start a business," the SBA says.

Next, divide essential expenses into two categories: fixed or variable. Fixed expenses might include monthly costs, such as rent, utilities, payroll, and insurance. Variable expenses might include inventory, shipping and packaging costs, and sales commissions. "The most effective way to calculate your startup costs is to use a worksheet that lists both one-time and ongoing costs," the SBA says.

―――――――――

Bootstrapping Tips

Nothing is scarcer than cash (except maybe sleep) when you're starting out. That's why the term "bootstrap"–i.e., doing more with less–is a buzzword in startup circles. The more you can bootstrap in the beginning to validate your business idea, the easier you are going to find your path to raising capital.

Tom Walker, an investor with Rev1 Ventures and author of *The Entrepreneur's Path: A Handbook for High-Growth Companies*, provides bootstrapping tips. Hold fixed costs to a minimum by doing the following:

- Share office services and equipment

- Co-locate with another company or move to a business incubator

- Use the computers and servers you already have

- Delay capital purchases

- Lease instead of purchase

- Negotiate fees and terms with all service providers and suppliers

Treat variable costs like you're spending your own money (which you are) by doing this:

- Seek trade credit terms with key suppliers

- Save thousands on travel by using smart scheduling or teleconferencing

- Hire interns from local business and/or design schools

SOURCE:
FRIENDS AND FAMILY

If anything puts family members' love to the test, it's asking them for money. Yet it happens every day. In fact, family and friends pour some $60 billion a year into startups, far more than professional investors. While Mom or Uncle Gene may be an excellent source of seed, the money almost always comes with strings attached. "It's the highest risk money you'll ever get," says David Deeds, who has taught entrepreneurship at Case Western Reserve University in Cleveland. "The venture may succeed or fail, but either way, you still have to go to Thanksgiving dinner."

Fortunately, there are ways to increase the odds that your relationships remain harmonious. A classic mistake is hitting up friends and family too early, before a formal business plan is in place, says Stephen Spinelli, who has served as director of the Arthur M. Blank Center for Entrepreneurship at Babson College.

No matter how excited you are about your idea, you need to be as rigorous as you would be if you were wooing the most jaded banker. That means supplying formal financial projections, as well as an evidence-based assessment of when your loved ones will see their money again. Why? For one thing, it lets your investors know that you think of their funds as something more than Monopoly money. And for another, it reduces the likelihood of unpleasant surprises.

On that note, we can't stress this enough: Make sure that your friends or family understand the real risks of investing in your startup. For that reason, avoid approaching people with little business knowledge, who may simply want to invest in your startup out of a sense of loyalty or altruism. Make sure your investors can afford to lose the money; it's not appropriate, for instance, for an older family member to sink their retirement savings into your startup.

Before you make the ask, think about how you want to structure the arrangement. Are you willing to give up equity? Or would you rather pay interest on a loan? The answers to these questions have major implications for both your business and your personal relationships.

Many entrepreneurs prefer debt, because it's cheaper over the long haul and involves no loss of control. Plus, you can deduct the interest as a business expense. On the other hand, if your business expects low cash flow for several years, or if you want to make your balance sheet look stronger because you're planning to borrow more money from an independent third party, a deal that involves equity could be preferable.

Some entrepreneurs have a relationship with friends and family where they can keep the terms fairly loose, categorizing the investment as an informal loan that will be paid back when the business has stable cash flow (which could take several years).

Whatever the terms, keep in mind that the investor usually comes attached to the cash. For instance, you may be peppered with questions every time you see your loved one. That's why you need to be careful, warns Deeds. "You want to get the right people onboard," he says. "The wrong investors can suck up an amazing amount of your time and force you to divert resources away from building the business."

Chris Baggott
and James Anderson

SITTING BEHIND HIS DESK at a marketing firm, Chris Baggott often daydreamed of owning his own business. In 1992, he finally took the plunge. At the age of thirty-one, he quit his job and bought Sanders Dry Cleaning, a local store that he eventually built into a chain with seven outlets. To make it happen, Baggott borrowed $45,000 from his father-in-law, James Twiford Anderson, a physician who also agreed to cosign a $600,000 bank loan.

With the financing in place, and ten years of marketing experience, Baggott thought he was set. And then the whole "business casual" trend caught fire. "People stopped wearing suits," Baggott recalls. Revenue fell to just $60,000 a month, far short of Baggott's original projections of $110,000. What's more, he owed $14,000 in monthly payments to the bank. Propping up the business with credit cards, he began missing loan payments—and the loan officer's phone calls went straight to his father-in-law. Says Baggott: "He'd call us and say, 'What the heck is going on here?' And then he'd have to write a check to cover it from his own funds."

Eventually, Baggott felt he had no choice but to sell the business, pay his debts, and move on. But there was one investor he couldn't repay: his father-in-law, who ultimately lost tens of thousands of dollars on the venture. "It was painful," Baggott says, though his father-in-law was "great" about it.

"You win some, lose some; it's trite to say, but it's true," Anderson told *Inc.* in a 2003 interview, adding that he knew from running his own practice and from some real estate ventures that things don't always go as planned. "I know whatever project Chris goes into, he puts his heart and soul into it."

Baggott eventually co-founded two software companies, Exact-Target in 2000 and Compendium in 2007. He again turned to friends and family—but this time, he went out of his way to emphasize the risk involved. "I said, 'Here's our business plan, but this is just a plan, and the chances are good that you'll never see this money again,'" he says.

Ultimately, he raised several million dollars—and investors once again included his father-in-law. This time, the support paid off: Salesforce bought ExactTarget in 2013 for $2.5 billion, while Oracle acquired Compendium for an undisclosed sum.

Baggott, who won an industry award called the TechPoint Trailblazer in Technology Award in 2015, publicly thanked Anderson for the support. Despite the early losses, "he was still the very first person to step up and help us get ExactTarget funded," Baggott recalled in his acceptance speech. "He was also an enthusiastic supporter of Compendium. So much for not mixing business and family—at least in our family, it's pretty much the same thing."

—

SOURCE:
CROWDFUNDING

Crowdfunding sites like Kickstarter and Indiegogo can be an effective way to raise money (and awareness) for your business idea, especially if it's a consumer product. Typically, you set a goal for how much money you'd like to raise over a period of time, say, $1,500 over forty days. Your friends, family, and strangers then use the site to pledge money. The sites have funded hundreds of thousands of creative ideas, from smartwatches to 3D printing pens. One of the more legendary success stories is that of Oculus, a virtual reality headset that raised $2.4 million via Kickstarter and was promptly acquired by Facebook for $2 billion.

The traditional way of crowdfunding is a system where your "backers" get a reward in return for their investment. For example, if you're trying to launch a new board game, you might send the game as a thank you to people who donate a certain amount of money. Campaigns on Kickstarter are all-or-nothing, meaning you get no funding unless you hit your target, although other sites have more flexible rules. Even if you fail to reach your financial goal, a crowdfunding campaign can be a potent marketing tool, helping you find and engage potential customers.

A newer and more complex type of crowdfunding is called *equity* crowdfunding. "With this model, people in the crowd are actually buying shares in the business. They're securing equity. They're investing in hopes of seeing a return," says Inc. columnist Steve Farber, founder of the Extreme Leadership Institute. "They want something more than a T-shirt." About 120 companies raised some level of money in 2016 using this method. Businesses like restaurants and microbreweries—those with strong brand loyalty that can quickly connect to a large crowd of customers and supporters—have been early adopters.

While you can raise up to $1 million through equity crowdfunding, it's not for everyone: You'll need anywhere from $8,000 to $15,000 in legal and setup costs. Platforms for equity crowdfunding include CircleUp and AngelList.

SOURCE:
BANK LOANS

It's never been easy for a small business to get a bank loan. Since the 2008 financial crisis, bankers are more risk-averse than ever. So, persuading one to take a shot on your small but growing company will take work.

A few rules of thumb: Don't expect to get a conventional bank loan on day one of your new business. (In the early years, you may have more luck with a Small Business Administration–backed loan. See "Make Mine an SBA Loan" on page 94). Do establish a track record, and keep careful paperwork. Don't ask for a bank loan when you're struggling to pay your bills. Do have a very good reason for why you need one. Some of the most common? Expanding into a new location, purchasing inventory or equipment, or boosting working capital.

The loan application process itself can be arduous. From start to finish, it can take two or three months—and you might get rejected in the end, says *Inc.* reporter Christine Lagorio-Chafkin. "It pays to be meticulous when you fill out your forms, and to provide ample documentation and back-up," she writes. "You should also plan on answering a series of questions both about your business and about your personal financial situation."

Because the application process is so important, let's take a look at how to go about it.

Chances are, you'll fill out several loan applications in a bid to get money. At the outset, you'll want to consider whether to target large national institutions with whom you might do other banking, or small, community-based organizations such as credit unions that might be more supportive of local entrepreneurs.

In either case, before beginning the application process, make sure you personally have good credit. A bank will also want to know if prior debts—both business and personal—will affect your ability to maintain a consistent payment schedule. "How you manage your personal finances is very reflective of how you might be able to manage business finances," says John E. Clarkin, a professor of entrepreneurship at the College of Charleston, South Carolina.

One area where many entrepreneurs are tripped up: Having too much personal credit. If you carry several credit cards in your wallet, each with a high level of available credit, a bank may worry that you might run into more debt by using that extra credit if the business runs into trouble.

Keep in mind, a lender will want to know the answers to these questions: Precisely why do you need a loan? If you intend to buy inventory or equipment, from whom will you buy it? Who at your company will manage the loan, if not you? Having a game plan to tackle these questions will make the process of filling out a loan application easier.

Most loan applications start with the basics: They ask for your business name and contact information, as well as the legal structure for your business (LLC or S corporation, for example), and the date of founding. You might also need to know how your business is covered under the North American Industry Classification System, commonly referred to as the NAICS code. (To learn more, go to the Census Bureau's website, www.census.gov.)

You'll also need to provide financial information, such as your current bank account (including recent deposits) and amount of income your business has earned in the past year, plus cash balance, debt payments, etc. Check with your accountant or financial advisor to make sure all your data is accurate. The bank will also want to know if you've paid your business taxes.

These days, lenders tend to ask small business owners for collateral or a personal guarantee—or to put up personal money should your business not be able to repay its loan. Weigh your options carefully. "You've got to be willing to lose some money, but don't endanger your entire future, your house, and your children's college education by pledging too much," says Dan Short, a professor of accounting at the Neeley School of Business at Texas Christian University.

The loan application will ask for additional personal information, including everything from a breakdown of the business's ownership (do you own 100 percent of the company, or do you share equity with other principals?) to whether you are married and filing the loan application jointly with your spouse. Additionally, you may be asked to provide personal tax information.

Make Mine an SBA Loan

➡️ Don't yet qualify for a bank loan? Enter the U.S. Small Business Administration.

The SBA supports America's small business owners through its various loan programs, helping entrepreneurs acquire the funds they need to get started and grow.

Contrary to what the term "SBA loan" suggests, the SBA actually doesn't directly lend the money to small businesses. Instead, the agency works with a number of lenders (see if your bank or credit union participates) around the country to guarantee a portion of the loans, providing a better incentive for lenders to approve small business loans.

One of the best-known recipients is Kevin Plank, founder of Under Armour, who received a $250,000 SBA loan in the early years of his athletic-apparel business. "I couldn't borrow any more money from friends or family or anybody else that I knew," he told the *Washington Post* in 2011. "I was out of options."

Here's a look at the SBA's most popular loan programs:

- **7(a) Loan.** The most commonly used of the SBA loans, the 7(a) loan is flexible in its terms and usage. Through the 7(a) program, small business owners can borrow up to $5 million to be used for working capital, equipment purchases, real estate, and some startup expenses. Under some conditions, business owners can use 7(a) loans to refinance pre-existing debt. Almost any small business owner is eligible for the 7(a) program, though qualification is up to intermediary lenders and will depend on your time in business, annual revenue, and personal credit score, among other factors.

- **Microloan.** The SBA offers very small loans (average size is $13,000) to new or growing small businesses. The money can be used for working capital or the purchase of inventory or equipment, but can't be used to refinance existing debt or purchase real estate. The SBA provides the funds to specially designated intermediary lenders, typically nonprofit community-based organizations with experience in lending as well as technical assistance. Some microlenders give priority to minority business owners, women, and low-income applicants in an effort to encourage entrepreneurship among these groups.

- **CDC/504.** The SBA CDC/504 Loan Program is designed for business owners making major tangible purchases, such as equipment, office space, and buildings. Though strictly regulated, CDC/504 loans are a powerful tool to help businesses grow in a decisive way. Borrowers (typically, "larger" small businesses) can take out up to $5 million to acquire or improve any fixed business asset. Think: opening a second location, making a major technological upgrade, or purchasing a large piece of real estate for development.

Lines of Credit Versus Traditional Loans

As a business owner, you might seek a business line of credit, which is similar to a personal line of credit, like a credit card or home-equity loan.

Unlike a traditional loan, which provides you with a lump sum of cash to be repaid at a fixed or variable interest rate over a certain time frame, the business line of credit allows you to tap into funds as you need them. This gives you control over how much money you take and when you take it. Additionally, you are only required to pay interest on what you use.

A business line of credit is commonly called revolving credit. This means the lender offers access to a certain amount of capital for an unspecified period. As payments are made, you get access to those funds back.

In some cases, a business line of credit may have lower interest rates and closing costs compared with a loan. But similar to a personal credit card, you may wind up paying more if you are late with a payment or go over your limit.

Typically, business owners seek out traditional term loans for specific purposes, such as the purchase of equipment that may take several years to pay off. A business line of credit may be better for short-term financing, such as payroll, supplier costs, or temporary cash-flow shortages.

SOURCE:
PROFESSIONAL INVESTORS

Very few startups will raise money from angel investors or venture capitalists—despite all those eye-popping headlines from Silicon Valley. By some estimates, fewer than 2 percent of entrepreneurs will receive cash infusions from professional investors. The more common sources of funding, by far, are personal savings and credit, followed by friends and family.

But if you're a cash-strapped entrepreneur with an idea that you think is the Next Big Thing, then equity financing—that is, selling shares in your company in return for capital—may be for you. Here's how these types of funding work.

Angels

Broadly defined, angel investors are high net-worth individuals who invest in entrepreneurial companies, usually at an early stage. Like institutional venture capital firms, many angel investors provide cash to young companies and take equity in return. One difference is that angel investors typically invest smaller amounts of money in individual companies than venture capitalists do, making them a possible resource for companies that have exhausted their "friends and family" financing options but are not ready to approach VCs for capital.

Some angel investors are members of angel groups, allowing them to increase their access to investment opportunities and giving them the possibility of investing jointly with other angels to hedge their risk. If you're looking for an angel, tapping into these networks (examples include New York Angels, Investors' Circle and Golden Seeds) is a good place to start. Also make use of your personal network—talk to entrepreneurs who have received angel funding, ask attorneys or accountants who deal in the venture field for referrals, and seek out connections by attending investment forums or pitch events. Your network may well be able to suggest potential angels.

In looking for angels to target, don't forget that choosing an angel investor is a great opportunity to gain an advisor. So, do your research. The best investor for your startup will be the one who can contribute significant experience, knowledge, and networking opportunities, as well as the cash you need to grow your business.

Keep in mind that there are drawbacks. When you take on an angel investor, you inevitably lose total control of your startup. An angel will want to ensure that his or her money is being spent wisely, and will likely take an active role in your company's decision making. In some cases, the angel will also want a board seat. You might also face new pressure to hit financial milestones. Before taking on an investor, make sure you feel comfortable that your company can grow at the rate the angel expects.

Many high-growth startups raise money from angels before going on to secure larger rounds of venture capital, which we'll outline next.

Venture Capital

Unlike angels who invest their own personal funds, venture capital firms pool cash from institutions or individuals into an investment fund, typically disbursing that money into any number of startups.

Since they have a fiduciary responsibility to partners, VCs generally don't like to make risky, early-stage investments. VCs often have larger sums to invest—in 2016, the median first or "Series A" round was about $6.6 million, according to Crunchbase. Because of the piles of cash being invested, venture capitalists can be demanding. Aside from taking a percentage of your company, VCs generally want to be actively involved in your company's strategic direction, taking board seats and sometimes managing operations. And they want an eventual exit strategy—an initial public offering, an acquisition, or some other event that promises a return on their investment.

Even if you're willing to give up all that control, venture capitalists are still quite picky about what companies they'll invest in. "One of the first hallmarks we look for is whether this is a high growth area or does this company have the potential for exceptional growth," says Maha Ibrahim, a general partner in Canaan Partners, a venture capital firm with offices in the United States and Israel. "We want to invest in companies that will grow by leaps and bounds over the next five-to-ten years so that it justifies going to the public market or provides an exceptional exit that creates enterprise value."

If you're looking for a VC, do your homework. Figure out firms' investment philosophies (often on their websites), the companies they have backed, and whether they invest at the early stage or later rounds. Talk to everyone you know who has been through the process of raising venture capital. And then tap into both your own and your management team's networks to find personal connections with your targets.

"The best way to get the attention of a potential venture capital investor for your startup is to have a mutual contact make an introduction by sending an executive summary/teaser document, which should be no longer than two pages," says attorney Lori Hoberman, whose New York City firm, Hoberman Law Group, advises entrepreneurs on how to navigate VC financing. "Remember, your intended audience has a very limited attention span. If they're interested after reading the executive summary, they'll come back to you for more."

If you do get a meeting, bring a prototype or a working model of your product. If interested, VCs will begin to conduct due diligence. Some companies perform due diligence on the product itself, hiring experts to examine the product or its market either from a technical standpoint or reviews from customers or potential customers.

The next step would be for the VC to issue a "term sheet," in which they make their financing offer. The term sheet will spell out the following:

→ The dollar amount of the investment the firm wants to make.

→ The level of ownership—basically a percentage of the company—they expect in return.

→ Other terms the VCs need to protect themselves, whether that includes board seats or conditions such as that the company cannot be acquired without the investors' approval.

Make sure to thoroughly review and evaluate term sheets before closing any deal. Most VCs will want regular progress reports after the documents are signed, and funding has been granted. "We tend to be involved in our companies but we don't want to micromanage," Ibrahim says. "It's a delicate balance." Companies should expect to make regular updates to investors. Often this is done at board meetings.

ALTERNATIVE FUNDING SOURCES

For entrepreneurs having trouble accessing traditional financing, there is an entire world of lending alternatives to help keep them afloat.

Once you start looking, "you'll realize alternative lenders have different standards than bank lenders do, and aren't necessarily looking for three years of perfect balance sheets," writes Inc.com reporter Jeremy Quittner. Many will focus on the potential your business has to grow, and will lend based on your future revenues or on the value of your other assets.

A word of caution: Do not jump into alternative lending blindly. "Rates can still be high and terms can be dubious," Quittner writes.

Here's a look at some of the options.

Factoring

Sure, factoring has a notoriously bad rap from the old days when factoring shops operated like sleazy used-car dealerships, where you'd risk sinking your business with usurious rates. But a lot has changed, and many reputable factors can lend you money at reasonable rates.

Factors lend you money by financing the value of your receivables, usually up to about 80 percent of their value. For that, they take on the task of bookkeeping and collecting plus any risk, such as the danger of a customer filing for bankruptcy.

In return, you get a loan that functions somewhat like a credit line. You'll be charged a commission for the credit, plus interest. The commission is likely to be about 1 percent of the total, and interest is likely to be prime plus about 3 percent. As a benchmark, rates on the SBA's guaranteed 7(a) loans range between prime plus 2.25 percent and prime plus 2.75 percent. Rates on non-guaranteed commercial loans will be even higher.

"Small businesses will come to a factoring institution because factors [unlike banks] are more focused on the collateral not the actual balance sheet," says Mike Stanley, managing director at Rosenthal & Rosenthal of New York, which factors for five hundred businesses, many in the small and mid-market.

Jonathan Levine is president of Lancer & Loader Group of New York, which for many years imported and distributed electronic consumer products. The company started distributing its LEDs to established retailers like Bed, Bath & Beyond, Costco, Sears, and Walmart in 2006. At the time no banks would lend, because the company couldn't provide several years of earnings, even though it had an impressive client roster.

Levine says he secured a $1 million credit line secured against receivables from Rosenthal & Rosenthal for rates comparable to a bank loan.

"Factoring is a good alternative for new companies who really need to focus their internal resources, both financial as well as human capital resources, toward growing the business," Levine says.

CIT, Rosenthal & Rosenthal, and Wells Fargo are three of the largest factors. You can also check out Factors Chain International, a network of over four hundred factors internationally, for more information.

Asset-Based Lending

This is similar to factoring, but instead of lending against outstanding invoices, lenders extend credit against the value of your assets. In some ways asset-based lending is similar to a bank loan, because unlike factoring, the lender does not take an active role in business collections.

An asset-based lender will go down the asset side of the balance sheet, assessing the value of items like inventory, equipment, machinery, real estate, and even intangible items like the worth of your name brand. It will then lend a percentage of the total value, usually up to 80 percent or more.

The asset-based lender takes a senior secured position in the loan, using the assets as collateral. Like traditional bank loans, asset-based loans have a closing fee between 0.5 percent and 1 percent of the total. All told, asset-based loans can be 1 to 3 percentage points higher than a bank loan, experts say.

Robison Oil of Elmsford, New York, found itself shut out of its bank's asset lending services when the bank pared back its energy division after a merger over ten years ago, says Dan Singer, a co-president of Robison. One of the things the bank was looking for was a strong balance sheet year after year. But since Robison is seasonal, it often showed a loss at the end of the year, which didn't fit its new bank's criteria.

It turned to Rosenthal & Rosenthal, which was willing to extend an $11 million term loan and $18 million credit line.

"We thought about going back to a bank, but we have found this segment of lenders much more flexible," Singer says, adding that total financing costs were about 1 percentage point more than the company would have gotten with a traditional bank loan.

Other asset-based lenders include Triton Financial Solutions and Simplified Leasing. Check out the Commercial Finance Association for more information on asset-based lending.

Nonbank Loans and Advances

A host of companies provide financing against future income. These companies have proliferated online since the banking crisis, but the loans tend be for smaller amounts. These are basically merchant advances secured against cash in the bank or potential credit card sales. One such lender, Kabbage, of Atlanta, does its underwriting over the web, looking at nontraditional criteria like PayPal information and number of sales on Etsy, as well as whether you communicate with customers on Facebook and Twitter. In that way, it compiles a credit score using alternate sources, unlike the credit score and credit bureau check that banks do, while considering the potential of your future business.

"Having more cash available is especially important in the online world when you have so many opportunities flowing by in a river and you have to scoop it up or it is gone," says Marc Gorlin, chairman and one of three co-founders of Kabbage.

Quick access to capital was important for Adam and Kit Chase, the owners of Trafalgarssquare.com, an online store for children's cards and wallpaper. The company was founded in 2008, and no bank would look seriously at it for financing, even though sales have been strong. In 2012, the Chases wanted to take advantage of a trend they had noticed in wall stickers and decals, for which they needed to buy special printing equipment.

"Banks had high interest rates, or they did not want to lend, or they were not flexible, they either wanted to give us an amount that was too large or too small," Kit Chase says.

Kabbage approved the Chases for a $2,000 loan, and the same day funds were in the couple's PayPal account.

"We have done a couple of things with flash sale sites, and often we won't have the money for materials, and with Kabbage we can get the money before events and produce products and pay it back," Kit Chase says.

Other similar providers include Lighter Capital and On Deck Capital. Amazon and PayPal also provide financing services to online merchants. A good resource to find a merchant advance lender is the North American Merchant Advance Association.

Loan Brokers

Brokers that specialize in small business loans can do the legwork of tracking down lending companies for you if you don't feel like doing this yourself. They can recommend a wide range of products and services, including things like merchant cash advances, accounts receivable and inventory financing, lease buybacks and purchase order financing, as well as more conventional loans like those offered by the SBA or even by the U.S. Department of Agriculture.

Such is the case for MultiFunding of Broad Axe, Pennsylvania, which checks these alternatives and others, for its clients.

"It is difficult for most small business owners today to know where they fit into the funding trajectory, there are so many moving parts," says Ami Kassar, chief executive of MultiFunding.

Generally speaking, small business owners consult with brokers at no cost, then pay a fee only if they successfully get financing. (In some cases, the broker charges the lender a fee.) Other online marketplaces include Biz2Credit, Fundera, and Lendio.

● ● ●

If there is anything more important than financing your young business, it's getting the word out about your new products or services. We'll take a look at a mix of marketing and sales strategies in the next chapter.

GET THE WORD OUT– AND GET CUSTOMERS

> " I was just really trying to find a fun, resonant way to tell the story of what our business did and why it existed."
>
> —
>
> **MICHAEL DUBIN,** founder of Dollar Shave Club, which used a now-famous YouTube video to introduce itself to a mass audience.

IN A PERFECT WORLD, YOU would have an unlimited budget to market your business in order to find new customers and increase sales. You could buy lots of online and offline advertising, run promotions to build traffic in store and online, and launch a proactive public relations campaign to increase your product or brand's visibility and awareness.

But this isn't a perfect world. Realistically, most small businesses and even many mid-sized firms have more great ideas on how to peddle their products than available resources.

So where do you start if you are looking to spread the word about your company? In this chapter, we'll show you how to maximize your visibility without draining your bank account.

MARKETING 101

Before you can find new customers and increase sales, you need to understand who your customer is, what value proposition you offer to customers, what your competition is currently offering in the market, and where there are gaps for a new entrant. In other words, you need to do some market research—whether that means hiring an outside firm to do the legwork or trying to do it yourself. (See "Conducting Market Research," page 113.)

"Attracting more customers is really about listening to their needs, not being a solution looking for a problem," says Paige Arnof-Fenn, founder and CEO of Mavens & Moguls, a strategic-marketing consulting firm. "There are many existing problems out there that need to be solved, that customers are willing to pay for."

When you understand your target audience, you can determine which key messages, features, and benefits matter to them. You can tell these customers how your business can help them solve their problems. For instance, "in order to have a customer go to your online shop, you have to find a reason why these customers want to come to you," says Jerry Osteryoung, who has served as director of outreach for the Jim Moran Institute for Global Entrepreneurship at Florida State University. "The value proposition has to be spelled out clearly."

Here are a variety of age-old staple techniques and newer tools you can use to reach these customers.

1. **Networking.** These days, most people blend traditional and online techniques. You can meet new contacts the old-fashioned way, by getting involved in community organizations such as the chamber of commerce, or by attending business functions such as trade shows, and then follow up via LinkedIn and Facebook. Social functions— dinner invitations, book clubs, golf outings, etc.—can lead

to potential business. Many businesses use online networks to make contacts through mutual friends or former colleagues.

2. **Referrals and reviews.** Here's where you develop champions of your products. Use business contacts who have been happy with your products to help generate references and referrals. Once you have sold to them, customers can help you sell to others by offering positive testimonials. You can also start a "refer-a-friend" campaign, encouraging referrals with rewards or discounts. This technique also employs word-of-mouth marketing. Encourage happy customers to post reviews on sites like Yelp (although make sure you don't offer incentives, which runs afoul of some review sites' rules).

3. **Affinity groups.** Look at noncompetitive products or services that are reaching out to the same audiences to see if there are ways you can collaborate through shared outreach efforts such as newsletters, mailings (online and offline), or co-branding opportunities. You probably can uncover a handful of like-minded products or services that are talking to your customers. Suggest to these business owners ways your businesses can support each other. Your customers will see joint efforts as a value-added opportunity to reinforce their choice of brands.

4. **Search engine optimization (SEO).** There are all sorts of tools through which you can drive potential new customers

to your website. SEO—using keywords and other techniques to make your site appear on the first page of listings on search engines—has become an art form. There are websites, such as Search Engine Watch, that will keep you updated about SEO strategies. There are, of course, paid SEO consultants who can help you with tricks and techniques, too. The top search engines are constantly updating their algorithms, so you need to monitor your website on a regular basis to make sure your keywords are leading customers to you. Make sure you are keeping your website up to date with fresh content so your customers come back often for more.

5. **Cold calling.** Most people (both the caller and the recipient) dislike cold calling, but there are ways to make it effective, says business coach Gordon Tredgold. "I appreciate that this may seem so obvious, but getting the right person on the line is critical, because your offer is only going to resonate and be relevant for the right customer," he says. "You need to do a bit of homework, check out their role, their responsibility—the better you can do this the more comfortable you're going to be making the call." He also recommends having a simple script and a clear objective that doesn't seem overly aggressive.

6. **Advertising.** Historically, businesses are encouraged to spend 3 to 5 percent of their revenue on advertising, but a small business needs to make sure that advertising is effective, Osteryoung says. One way to do this is to ask your cus-

tomers where they heard about you so that you can measure what is effective. In addition, carefully pick your markets for advertising to make sure you're reaching your target audience. If you're targeting an older audience, print ads might still be the way to go. But if it's Gen X or millennials you're after, you may be better off advertising online. Google's advertising system (AdWords), still the dominant player, requires time and money—but businesses of all types and sizes say it's time and money well spent. Social media (more on that shortly) is supposed to be free—and it is—but "boosting" a post on Facebook or promoting a tweet can greatly increase your reach and bring new customers and followers.

Conducting Market Research

 Market research runs the gamut from very simple qualitative research to in-depth quantitative analysis.

It can be done very quickly and inexpensively by sending surveys to your existing or potential customers using one of the many online survey tools, such as SurveyMonkey. You can also get to know the target audience by looking at existing sources of information—from the U.S. Census Bureau or other government agencies, from trade associations, or from third-party research firms.

Depending on the questions you are trying to answer and your research budget, your market research can involve more extensive interviews with customers and qualitative studies on how target customers feel about your business, its products, and its services.

Certain products and services may appeal to one audience but not to another, so understanding the strengths, weaknesses, opportunities, and threats in your target market is critical. You can get to know your customers and segment the market any number of ways including by:

- Demographics—statistical data on a population including income levels, age, etc.

- Psychographics—the attitudes and tastes of a certain demographic.

- Ethnographics—examination of particular cultures.

- Buying habits—how, what, and where customers purchase products and services.

———————

DigitalOcean

IF YOU'RE THE AVERAGE consumer, you may not have heard of DigitalOcean, a cloud hosting site for developers. But here's why it's an interesting case study: The site has grown exponentially since its 2011 launch, raising $123 million from investors and registering nearly a million users.

Mitch Wainer, DigitalOcean's chief marketing officer, says the company expanded through a series of marketing hacks, outlined below, which other businesses can use.

First, he recommends inviting a core group of customers to try out a "beta" or early version of your product or service. In DigitalOcean's case, the startup demonstrated its first product at a New York tech meetup—the perfect place to find its developer customers. It signed up fifty. Wainer says he followed up with phone conversations with those early adopters, asking them a variety of questions about their favorite foods or books or blogs. The point? To come up with a blueprint of a typical customer—a key to targeting the rest.

After that, he says he allocated a small marketing budget for getting more customers. You may be bootstrapping, but getting the world to find your product or service isn't going to happen without a bit of investment, he says. Set goals, such as doubling your users or customers within thirty days. "Whatever it is, you want to set targets and goals month over month, and you want to be tracking day to day," he says.

As an online business, Wainer says he found discounts or promo codes—distributed via website banner and text ads—to be highly effective. "We used BuySellAds.com and BuyAds.com to find relevant websites to place a banner ad on," he says.

In the beginning, it's important to closely monitor every online marketing campaign you set in motion to understand what's most effective in getting people to sign up or take action. Wainer suggests creating monthly key performance indicator (KPI) reports, an easy thing to do with a simple spreadsheet populated with data from Google Analytics as well your conversion data. "You want to build monthly reports to track your channels and your spending," he says.

DigitalOcean also tried so-called content marketing, providing programming tutorials on its site to build credibility and attract customers. Wainer recommends that startups aim for about twenty posts per month of content, hiring a writer if need be.

As a tech startup, DigitalOcean was able to quadruple its number of users by "A/B testing," or comparing versions of things like call-to-action buttons, pricing models, and messaging to see which was most effective, he says. But any company can play with pricing or offerings. He also recommends refer-a-friend campaigns (he used a referral automation tool called Ambassador) and contests to give existing customers an incentive to sign up more customers.

DigitalOcean also used Facebook and Twitter ads to spread the word about its product. On Twitter, for example, the company pinpointed key "influencers"—people who have the power to affect the buying decisions of others—retweeting them to get on their radar. "Those relationships build more awareness and spread [your product or service] via word of mouth," he says.

Lastly, the company used MailChimp and Campaign Monitor for help with email campaigns. If customers dropped the service, Wainer says DigitalOcean sent automatic emails from the CEO, asking for feedback and crediting their accounts, which led some customers to reactivate.

—

SOCIAL MEDIA 101

Social media marketing has become an essential part of every modern company's marketing plan (and if it's not, it needs to be). The bottom line: If your customers are on social media, then you need to be, too.

Most entrepreneurs know they need to get in the social game, yet there are so many networks—and they evolve so rapidly—that it's difficult to know where to focus your efforts. This is especially true for budget-strapped smaller businesses that can't afford to give each one a test drive.

Keep in mind, you can use social media in a variety of ways. If you don't wish to spend any money, you can simply share content—whether that's text updates, photographs, or videos—for free, to an audience of followers. If budget allows, you can choose to use your social-media platform as an advertising vehicle, paying small amounts to boost or promote your content, or spending major dollars for full-scale campaigns.

Here is a quick set of considerations as you select the best social network(s) for your business:

Facebook is right for you...if you are building a community presence or want to reach as broad a network as possible. It is losing some traction among younger users but remains the most popular social media site by far. "Not only does it have the most users, it is the most frequently used, which demonstrates a high level of engagement," says Michelle Manafy, editorial director of Digital Content Next, a trade association. Sheer popularity may not be your primary criteria, however. Given that the primary reason people are so engaged with Facebook is to connect with family and friends, it may not provide the most effective medium for your business message.

LinkedIn is right for you...if you are in B2B or in another industry or role in which you can provide useful insights to people thinking about their work, seeking to make business connections, or looking for their next job. "While LinkedIn is trying to broaden the scope of its information, most users are in work mode on LinkedIn so it is optimal for peer networking and industry-specific information," Manafy says. The average LinkedIn user tends to have a higher income and education level than that of other networks, she adds.

Instagram is right for you...if you have a visual aspect to what you do, as it is primarily a photo- and video-sharing app. Instagram appeals to urbanites and younger consumers who are on-the-go, as posts to Instagram can only be made with a mobile device. Sentiment on Instagram also tends to be more positive than platforms such as YouTube, where snarky comments tend to be the norm, says Corbett Drummey, CEO of Popular Pays, a Chicago company that helps brands run social-media campaigns.

Twitter is right for you...if you want to reach both male and female customers, and especially "information junkies," as the microblogging site lends itself to topic-based news or timely insights. As with Facebook, Twitter is more effective when it is a two-way platform in which you respond to and engage with followers.

Pinterest is right for you...if you are in a highly visual industry with customers who will naturally seek to express themselves through images. It's the ideal medium for any company that wants to sell fashion, home products, or other things to women sitting at their computers, Drummey says.

Snapchat is right for you...if you are trying to target younger audiences or engage with millennials. That said, it tends to be more popular with well-known brands trying to stay relevant, as opposed to startups trying to win new customers, Drummey says. If you choose Snapchat, remember: Most of your content will disappear quickly, so you'll need a lot of it. On the bright side, posts don't need to be immaculately edited, so it's a good platform if you want to share behind-the-scenes or "day-in-the-life" posts.

YouTube is right for you...if you or your business aims to share tutorials and DIY videos aimed at niche audiences. A warning: "It's not great for sentiment," Drummey says. "YouTube comments are kind of like the gutter of the Internet sometimes." But for new brands, or those struggling to stand out in crowded markets, viral videos can be the ultimate way to increase exposure and drive traffic.

BEST PRACTICES FOR SOCIAL MEDIA PROMOTION

Let's talk data. The average person spends 118 minutes a day on social media sites like Facebook (which boasts more than 1.5 billion active users worldwide), Twitter, Instagram, and Snapchat, while 74 percent of consumers rely on social media to influence their buying decisions.

"Quite simply, if your brand isn't using social media to the fullest extent possible, there's a good chance you're missing out on potential sales," says Sujan Patel, co-founder of growth marketing agency Web Profits.

Marketing on social media doesn't have to be scary—and you don't have to do it all at once. You just have to start. Patel recommends keeping the following best practices in mind as you begin promotions on any social network. "Use them to improve brand recognition, build a loyal customer base, and drive more sales with social media," he says.

Post meaningful content. Red Mango, a popular frozen yogurt chain, shares customer reviews, pictures, and product information on Facebook, Instagram, and Twitter. A typical photo posted mid-week on Facebook might depict a banana peanut butter smoothie, with the caption "Hump day fuel." The chain uses social media to keep customers updated on menu changes and seasonal offerings, while also giving followers the opportunity to interact with the brand.

Keep your branding consistent. Making the effort to keep your messages uniform can help you cultivate a loyal customer following. Multiple representations can get confusing. If the branding and image you're cultivating is too different across platforms, customers may question whether it's coming from the same company.

Use hashtags appropriately. Don't go overboard, and don't try to get too clever. For example, Domino's Pizza started the campaign #letsdolunch to advertise a sale in their UK-based restaurants. The simplicity of the hashtag made it easy for people to remember and allowed the campaign to catch on with the general public.

Don't overload your profiles with sales messages. Nobody wants to feel like they're more prospect than brand loyalist. Watch your engagement data to target prime posting times and avoid oversharing.

SALES 101

“ There has never been a business that succeeded without sales."

MARK CUBAN, serial entrepreneur, owner of the NBA's Dallas Mavericks, and shark on ABC's *Shark Tank*

The purpose of any business is to bring in customers. For a newbie owner, that can be harder than it sounds if you don't have any sales experience.

Most entrepreneurs start a company because they're excited about a product or a service, not because they're excellent salespeople. In fact, many have never worked in sales. The good news is that you can learn (and even enjoy) the art of selling, with a bit of practice. At its most basic level, selling is simply explaining to someone the *logic* and *benefits* of buying your product or service.

Keep in mind, sales skills can be used for far more than landing customers. You can use sales skills to win financing, bring on partners, hire key employees, or line up distribution deals.

Jeff Haden, an Inc.com columnist, asked about twenty business owners and CEOs to name the one skill they feel contributes the most to their success. What did every one of them say? "Sales skills," he says. "They all felt success is almost impossible—in any field—without solid sales skills."

But learning to embrace salesmanship can be tricky for people. Not only does the word "sales" conjure up slick and unsavory techniques, but it can also trigger a fear of rejection.

"If you represent a product, you probably use it yourself and believe in it with all your heart," says Marla Tabaka, a small-business advisor. "And those of you who are inventors have poured blood, sweat, and tears into developing your products, not to mention tons of money." For service providers, the thought of rejection is especially daunting because your personal knowledge and talent are literally your stocks in trade. "All of these scenarios make it only natural to embrace your business as an extension of your very being," she says. "Hearing *no* can feel like a very personal rejection."

We asked experts for their best tips on how to get outside your comfort zone and learn to sell with success:

→ **Face it, you're a salesperson.** Just like everyone else. "So many people resist the fact that they are salespeople," says Connie Kadansky, a sales coach at Sales Call Reluctance with twenty years of experience. "They've had experience with salespeople who were less than professional." If you think about it, she says, a salesperson is someone who solves problems for a profit. Look at it that way, and just about everyone you know is in sales.

→ **Believe in your own value.** You have value as an individual, and the product or service you're selling creates great value as well when matched with the right customer. "When people are convinced of their value, they're unstoppable," Kadansky says. "If someone on the other end is discourteous or not receptive, it doesn't faze them." (If you don't believe what you're selling has real value, you should be selling something else.)

→ **Know your material cold.** "Whatever you're selling, you have to know that product or service up and down, inside and out," says Ravin Gandhi, co-founder of GMM Nonstick Coatings, a supplier to the housewares industry. Anticipate questions in advance, and determine ahead of time what your clients' wants or needs are. Kadansky suggests preparing a script, focused on the client, not on you. "'Many companies similar to yours count on me to...' fill in the blank," she says.

→ **Remember, it's all about relationship building.** Keep that in mind before a cold call, says Tabaka, when fear of rejection can be particularly high. "Sometimes we put the pressure on by thinking that our cold calls should result in sales," she says. Instead, remember that a goal is simply to make contact. You might come up with a plan to contact prospects at a later date, when they may be in need of your service or product. If someone isn't initially interested, it doesn't mean "that they don't like you or your product," she says. "It simply means that it's not right for them at this time."

→ **Be a good listener.** Don't try to push. "A great way to build a rapport with your clients is to just listen to what they say," Gandhi says. "Most of the time your clients will actually tell you what they want and all you have to do is deliver." All too often, entrepreneurs get so wrapped up in what they can offer that they forget to listen to what their prospective customers need. "Every opportunity with a new prospect should be centered on their needs, what they do, whom they sell to, and any personal or business goals they are currently focused on," says Inc.com columnist Barry Farber, a sales strategist.

→ **Don't forget to follow up.** Write an email or letter to your sales prospect immediately following your first promising meeting, summarizing what was discussed, highlighting the benefits of what you can provide, and listing the actions to follow (which could be the next time you plan to speak). Not only does this demonstrate that you listened, it will be a good reference point down the road, when your prospect inevitably needs a nudge. "If thirty days goes by and nothing happens, you can follow up" by referring to the initial letter, Gandhi says.

→ **Learn to be persistent.** "Salespeople hear the word *no* all the time," Haden says. "Over time you'll start to see *no* as a challenge, not a rejection. And you'll figure out what to do next." Try to remove the emotion by seeing your phone calls and meetings as statistics, Tabaka says. If you make twenty-five phone calls, odds are good that you will find one person who will want to learn more. "It's like working up to a hundred sit-ups instead of staying at twenty," she says. "Get those numbers up there; love the *no* because it only means that you are getting closer to the *yes*."

Still worried about your sales skills? "If you're a would-be entrepreneur, set aside your business plan and work in sales for a year or two," Haden recommends. If you're struggling to keep your business afloat, consider a part-time sales job to bring in extra income and gain some much-needed sales experience. One reason you might be struggling is because of poor sales skills.

"Go learn how to sell," Haden says. "It's the best investment you will ever make."

FIVE POWERFUL SALES TECHNIQUES

David Finkel, a business author and Inc.com columnist, says he often gets this question at business conferences: "Which five sales techniques would you use more than any others?"

His answer is below. The list spells out favorite approaches that he has used for over twenty years while selling products and services to consumer and business-to-business clients, from short sales cycles of less than twenty-four hours to long sales cycles of twenty-four months. "They flat out work," he says.

1. **Magnify the pain and make the cost real, present, and unbearable.** How do you do this? By asking questions and helping your prospect articulate the real cost of their status quo. Here are some questions that will help.

   "Tell me about your current situation..."

   "What's not working right now...?"

   "Tell me more..."

   "What is the real impact...?"

   "What happens if you don't deal with this and find a solution?"

   "And what is that going to cost you?"

   "Why is it you're finally dealing with this now? I mean, what sparked that need to fix the situation now versus just living with it for another year?"

2. **Create scarcity and tap into the fear of loss.** Nothing prompts action like the competitive urge. It is hard-wired deep into your prospect's brain. How can you appropriately inject competition into the conversation with your prospect?

   "Mike, you shared that it is important that you get delivery and installation by the first of next month. If that is

the case I just need to bring up that I would need to get
the PO ASAP because we're entering into a busy season
and our installation team is booked heavy."

Or...

"Sharon, we can only work with one client in this area
because of the standard non-compete we sign with any
client. From your perspective, why is it you think we
should pick your company to partner with in Tampa?"

3. **Preempt your top two sales objections.** What objections
   do you hear over and over again? Rather than let the objections come up and then overcoming them with brute force,
   preempt them. Address and dissolve them before they are
   articulated by your prospect. This could be through the use
   of a selling story, a better frame for the sale, or some other
   scripted mechanism.

4. **Save a key sales objection to the end, and use that as a**
   lever to close the sale. It can often be a powerful sales
   closing technique to "close on the objection." Here is what
   it might sound like:

   Prospect: "But we need the cost to be under $4,000 per
   unit."

   You: "So I'm hearing that you need the unit cost to be un-
   der $4,000. May I ask why this is so important for you?"

   Prospect: "Because otherwise we'll be over our budget
   since we need twelve units."

You: "Got it. Assuming we could get you that pricing, and I'm not sure we can, but assuming we could, is there anything else that would stop you from moving forward with the purchase? Or no, if you got that pricing you'd definitely move forward with this?"

Notice what you're doing is fleshing out any other objections before you work to solve that final one, and making it clear that they have bought contingent on solving that last objection.

"When you know you have a key objection, sometimes it can make strategic sales sense to leave it until the end and use that objection to create the emotion and movement to close the deal," Finkel says.

5. **Help prospects sell themselves.** This technique is also called Aikido selling, after the Japanese martial art, and the concept is that you "blend energies" with your prospect. In other words, you don't sell in the sense that you need to convince or talk somebody into anything. "The best salesperson helps her prospect close himself," Finkel says. "You do this through asking great questions that build customer motivation, and restating and reframing your prospect's responses to help them sell themselves."

Dollar Shave Club

MICHAEL DUBIN IS THE founder of Dollar Shave Club, the Venice, California, razor-delivery service that got its first big boost from a 2012 YouTube video in which Dubin stars.

The video, which went supernova-viral in seventy-two hours, took a day to shoot and cost about $4,500. It helped that Dubin used to do improv and sketch comedy in New York before founding Dollar Shave Club in 2011.

"I know humor is a very powerful device in telling a story," he says. The video features Dubin, among other things, dancing with a giant bear, riding with an "employee" in a tiny red wagon, and blowing dollar bills with a leaf blower. "I was just really trying to find a fun, resonant way to tell the story of what our business did and why it existed."

Dollar Shave Club was strategic in releasing the video, timing it to an announcement that the company had secured $1 million in seed money and that it had relaunched its site. "All the usual suspects [such as niche sites like TechCrunch] covered the three events," Dubin says. "From there, the mainstream media picked up on them, and the video took off."

The events were also designed to coincide with South by Southwest, the major festival in Austin, Texas, that draws thousands of entrepreneurs, investors, and startups. "Everyone was talking about the video while they were in Austin, so strategically it ended up being a pretty smart move," he says.

By 2017, the video had been viewed about 25 million times. And Dollar Shave Club? It was purchased by Unilever for $1 billion in 2016.

—

HIRING YOUR FIRST SALES REP

We've looked at how to improve your sales skills in the early stages of your startup.

But once you've gotten your business off the ground, you might consider hiring your first sales reps. Many founders make this decision because they want to increase sales and enter new markets—and, truth be told, they're tired of working seventy-hour weeks.

Some businesses will start by hiring independent sales reps (please see "How to Find Independent Sales Reps," page 138). Others will want to hire and train an internal sales force. The latter option will take more time and resources, but may pay off down the road, as your employees will be focused exclusively on your products or services.

We'll take a look below at how to hire internal sales reps. To ensure these new team members will be a worthwhile investment for your company, *Inc.* columnist Geoffrey James recommends doing the following:

1. **Examine your sales process.** If you're ready to hire somebody to sell, you've likely already acquired some customers. While some of that business may have come from previous business contacts, you've probably got some idea of what it takes, in terms of expertise and skill set, to sell your offering. Make a list of what's required, such as "knowledge of manufacturing processes" or "experience selling to large corporations."

2. **Interview your existing customers.** Many entrepreneurs forget this part, hiring sales reps without asking their customers how they want vendors to sell to them. The more you find out about the environment in which your sales rep will be selling, the better you'll be able to decide whether a particular candidate is right for the job. And by the way: Your customers will be pleased that you bothered to ask.

3. **Write a concise job description.** Make it specific, not general. Some examples:

   → "The job requires interaction with these customer types: [IT director, etc.]."

   → "The job requires telephone cold calling, generating at least ten sales leads a day."

   → "The job requires the ability to build a network of customer advocates."

Your goal here is to define the job clearly, without jargon.

4. **Devise a reasonable compensation plan.** Probably the biggest mistake that small business owners make when hiring salespeople is underestimating the amount of effort it's going to take to sell their offerings. "If you truly believe (as many entrepreneurs do) that your product or service will 'sell itself,' then you probably shouldn't be thinking about hiring a salesperson—not because you don't need one, but because you're fooling yourself," James says.

5. **Use your own network.** Now that you've got your concise job description, contact everyone you know who might know somebody who has those characteristics. In fact, the process of writing the job description may have brought somebody to mind. A personal referral from a colleague is much more likely to yield a great candidate than somebody who answers an advertisement.

6. **Contact your local business school.** While not all business schools have sales courses or programs, they're becoming more popular. "The graduates from such programs have an incredibly high success rate compared to other kinds of sales new hires and are often exposed to a broader range of business concepts," says Howard Stevens, CEO of Chally Worldwide, a sales consulting firm.

7. **Run ads.** If steps 5 and 6 have come up blank, then run ads on job boards and industry publications. Since you wrote a very specific job description, "you're less likely to get deluged with plain-wrap resumes from every Tom, Dick, and Mary who's 'highly motivated' and 'success driven,'" James says.

8. **Interview to determine character.** When you call somebody in for an interview, you already know (from your description and the response) that they've got the basic attributes you need. Now your primary job is to assess character. "Try to find employees whose personal experience illustrates the kind of resilience that will help them shrug off the inevitable disappointments that are part of

any career in sales," advises Gerhard Gschwandtner, publisher of *SellingPower* magazine.

9. **Do your due diligence.** Unless you're hiring somebody with no prior sales experience, the interview should cover how much the candidate sold in his or her previous position. Ask the candidate about compensation for those sales. Try to find somebody who worked with the candidate in the past, other than the references that he or she provided. (LinkedIn can be a good resource for this.) If you find any inconsistencies, disqualify the candidate.

10. **Hire conditionally, on a trial period.** "The truth is that you don't really know if a sales professional is going to work out until after they've attempted to sell for you," James says. Large companies typically have formal trial periods for sales reps, but smaller firms may not be accustomed to thinking about hiring in this way. Make sure that you have precise (i.e., numerical) measurements for what constitutes success.

FiveStars

VICTOR HO KNOWS A lot about hiring sales staff. Shortly after co-founding FiveStars, a loyalty program platform for small businesses, he made the decision to triple the startup's sales team, hiring a hundred reps. The strategy paid off, with the San Francisco company adding merchants (its paying customers) five times faster than before.

Ho says he followed certain rules in order to build a sales force rapidly but successfully. For starters, he only hired reps whose experience specifically matched the job. He resisted the temptation to hire star reps whose skills didn't fit, even if they had incredible track records.

"We don't want to hire people and churn and burn them as other sales organizations sometimes do," Ho explains. "We will pass on somebody if we don't think we have the structure that will make that person successful."

As FiveStars quickly grew, Ho says the company made training a priority, with top managers and founders spending two to four hours a month training new hires. "This investment in training to reduce ramp time is particularly valuable in sales," Ho says.

The company also had some of its most experienced and successful sales reps devote all their time to training new hires. "Most companies wouldn't tell their best sales reps to stop selling and focus on training," Ho says. "But for us, making sure every individual rep is set up to succeed will end up being the best for the company."

That's also why the company only hired as many reps as it could train—the right way.

"When designing our onboarding system, we prioritized scaling our culture and keeping the training personalized and engaging," Ho says. The company decided to limit each new "class" of sales reps to fifteen, to maintain an intimate feel.

Most companies would figure out how many people they wanted to hire and then design a training system around that target, he adds. But he believes cultivating the right experience is too important. "People are coming out of onboarding with solid knowledge of our founders, our products, and how we talk about the company," he says.

As FiveStars expanded into new markets, Ho says he never wanted sales offices to feel cut off or removed from the center of the action. So, when the company opened a new sales office in Denver, one of the founders actually moved to Denver for six months to be on hand while the new office got up and running. "It's a big mistake to treat a new office as an extension," he says.

Thanks in part to an investment in its sales staff, FiveStars secured nearly $100 million in financing in 2016. It plans to use the funds to build its brand and business across the United States.

—

How to Find Independent Sales Reps

➡ You want to bring your new product to market as quickly as possible, but you're on a tight budget. You don't want to spend the time or the money putting together a sales team, so what are your options?

One consideration is working with independent sales representatives—sometimes called manufacturers' representatives or manufacturers' agents—who sell products or services to customers directly for the company or companies he or she works for.

Reps typically work as commission-only independent contractors, so there's generally no initial risk in hiring them. But you may have to dole out a higher commission for each sale. That might be worth the price if you want to test the market, or if your product will benefit from a demonstration or your customers require constant explanation of new products.

One place to look is a rep-matching service like RepHunter. net or RepRight.com. Or visit well-known trade shows to meet with independent agents. You can also search for independent sales reps on LinkedIn. Depending on your industry, typical commission rates run anywhere from 5 to 25 percent of the sale, according to the Manufacturers' Agents National Association.

• • •

In this chapter, we looked at a variety of marketing and sales techniques you can use to spread the word about your initial products and services. In the pages ahead, we'll take a look at next steps, including getting to truly know your customers, and staying innovative so you can continue to meet their wants and needs.

DIG DEEP TO DISCOVER CUSTOMERS' WANTS AND NEEDS

> " You can't just ask customers what they want and then try to give that to them. By the time you get it built, they'll want something new."

STEVE JOBS, Apple co-founder.

IT MAY BE STATING THE obvious, but you'll grow your company most successfully when you are able to solve the problems of your customers like no other.

Perhaps the person who knew his customers the best was Apple co-founder Steve Jobs, who repeatedly launched user-friendly products that solved basic problems people were having (or one might argue, didn't even know they were having yet) with computers, phones, and other devices.

To anticipate customers' needs, first you'll need to know them better than they know themselves. "You need to know them as well as you know your best friends, your significant other, or your family members," says Sonia Thompson, a small-business advisor.

When you have this familiarity with your customers, it enables you to continue to design the products and services they will buy— and it allows you to "create a delightful experience that keeps them coming back for more," Thompson says.

Customer familiarity is a unique advantage that many small startups have, especially in the early years. Big companies like

Walmart and Amazon excel in operational excellence, and innovative businesses like Tesla, Starbucks, and Nike focus their energy on product leadership. But as an entrepreneur, customer intimacy is your domain.

> **"** When I was still a stay-at-home mom, I started a mobile blow-dry business, traveling to people's homes. I'd usually set up in the kitchen or living room, which meant the women weren't seated in front of a mirror. There was always this moment at the end when they'd go running to see their hair and let out this big squeal. When I opened a physical location, I knew I wanted to re-create that moment and the excitement of the reveal."
>
> **ALLI WEBB,** co-founder of Drybar, now a nationwide retail chain of seventy-four salons, where mirrors are placed behind customers

That said, predicting what will appeal to customers—and what will trigger them to buy—can be tricky. "The number one worry we hear from our clients today is this: 'I need to understand my customer better, but it's getting harder, not easier,'" says Paul J. H. Schoemaker, founder of Decision Strategies International Inc., a strategic management consulting firm.

Why is getting a handle on customers' wants and needs an increasingly hard proposition for so many entrepreneurs? Here are some of the reasons, according to Schoemaker, who is also a senior fellow at the Mack Institute for Innovation Management at the University of Pennsylvania's Wharton School:

→ Customers are less loyal and far less trusting than they used to be. This is especially true in industries whose reputations suffered during the 2008 financial crisis—including banking, pharmaceuticals, energy, airlines, and media. But even if you're in an unrelated industry (and most startups are) you're likely to feel some of the same effect.

→ Consumers are more demanding and have more power than ever before, thanks to social media, easy online comparison-shopping, and a proliferation of choices.

→ Customers are more diverse than ever, making it harder for entrepreneurs to identify their characteristics.

→ The data deluge brought on by the Internet has caused an overload, making it more difficult for businesses to understand customers. (Data overload confuses customers as well.)

→ Thanks to technology, many startups conduct business entirely online, in effect serving customers they never actually "meet."

UNDERSTANDING YOUR AUDIENCE

Who are your customers? What do they care about? What stresses them out and keeps them up late on a Tuesday night? What are their goals for this quarter? What tools and software are they already using, and what are they not using? How do they talk with their colleagues, and what do they talk about most?

If you don't know the answers to all those questions, never fear: There are ways to find out. And it may not be as difficult (or as privacy-invading) as you might think.

> **"** I do most of my grocery shopping at a place called Olivia's Market, a small grocer in my neighborhood. I've gotten to know the owner, Bill Maheras, fairly well. Bill always tells me how lucky I am to run a software company. With high margins, no spoilage, and no inventory, our businesses are polar opposites. But I always remind Bill how in at least one respect, he is far luckier than I: He actually knows his customers. In today's hundred-data-points-on-your-customer world of online business, Bill has one data point that really matters: He can recognize a customer if he sees her walking down the street. Can you say that about your company? I know I can't."
>
> **JASON FRIED,** co-founder of Basecamp, which makes team communication software

Here are a few easy exercises that can help you and your growing company understand your audience:

→ **Stand in your customer's shoes.** "Look beyond your core business and understand your customer's full range of choices, as well as his or her ecosystem of suppliers, partners, etc.—of which you may be part," suggests Schoemaker. This exercise will also deepen your understanding of competitors and help you better anticipate their moves.

→ **Staple yourself to a customer's order.** "Track key customers' experiences as they traverse your company's pathways and note anyplace where the experience breaks down," he says. Some hospitals ask interns to experience the check-in process as fake patients. Some founders (like Jessica Alba of Honest Co.) listen in on customer-service calls. If you can't exactly put yourself through a customer experience, try role-playing exercises at all points of the customer's experience with your company.

→ **Field diverse customer teams.** IBM, for instance, sends senior teams from different disciplines into the field to meet customers and develop a deep understanding of how to serve them better, Schoemaker says. Another company might add members of its back-office support group to its customer team, supplementing the usual customer-facing roles.

→ **Learn together with customers.** Another example from the corporate world: GE invited its top customers in China, along with local executives and account managers, to a seminar on leadership and innovation. Doing so not only helped GE executives better understand the mindset of Chinese counterparts; it also helped them *influence* that mindset. Consider whether there is an event or workshop you can host for your customers.

But how do you truly anticipate what customers will want tomorrow, as Steve Jobs did so exquisitely? And how do you continue to innovate—so that your customers will continue to choose your products or services for years to come?

ANTICIPATING YOUR CUSTOMER'S NEEDS

Like it or not, your industry is changing—and that means, of course, that your customers' needs are changing, too. "Everything changes; it always has, and it always will," says John Hall, founder of Influence & Co, a content marketing agency. "You can keep up with and be part of the changes, or you can overlook and ignore changes and let others pass you by."

There are countless examples of companies that missed the early warning signs of impending change. Coors failed to see the trend toward low-carb beer until it was almost too late. Blockbuster belatedly introduced a rentals-by-mail and streaming service to fight against Netflix; it filed for bankruptcy protection in 2010. Lego responded poorly to the electronic revolution in toys and gaming, and then went on to underestimate the squeeze that Walmart and China would put on its pricing power. (Happily, Lego made a comeback in the late 2000s; see case study on page 162.)

It's not always easy to keep up with what's trending in your industry, or what's shifting in your field, but doing so can help forecast what customers will want to buy in the future. Here are seven ways you can identify and evolve with trends in your industry:

1. **Take advantage of industry research and trends reports.** One of the simplest things you can do to better recognize trends is to read the latest reports or white papers. Often, industry leaders perform original research and compile their findings in one large report. By taking the time to read through it (beyond the executive summary), you can generally find information that's valuable and relevant to what's trending in your space.

   For example, "As the CEO of a content marketing agency, I like following a variety of marketing reports to stay on top of trends," Hall says. He keeps up on the latest in content marketing by reading Content Marketing Institute's research reports, and by digging through Information Technology Services Marketing Association's report library. "These reports don't contain the word of God or anything, but reading a variety of reports can help you get a feel for the landscape and where things are headed," he says.

2. **Regularly follow publications and influencers in your industry.** If you're like most time-pressed entrepreneurs,

you probably don't have the time (or desire) to read through every interesting report a leader in your space produces. If you aren't up for the long read, a good alternative is to peruse top blogs and publications in your industry, every day. Many will reference data from the longer reports, allowing you to still gather that information but in a more conversational, easy-to-digest format.

3. **Use tools and analytics to identify the direction trends are heading.** Depending on your industry, your audience, your goals, and even the size of your company, different tools and metrics will be important to you to identify trends.

   "Fortunately for me, when I look at things like Google Trends, I can see from a big-picture perspective that the area my company specializes in—thought leadership—is steadily increasing in search interest," Hall says. His marketing team uses tools like Google AdWords and Moz to better pinpoint the exact keywords and queries that potential customers use in searches. "From there, we can analyze the big picture and the smaller picture to evolve with those trends," he says.

   Whatever your industry, it's important to use a variety of tools together (from Google to your CRM system to a customizable analytics template) to track your customers' behavior, identify any correlations among a specific audience, and monitor your performance.

What's CRM?

CRM stands for customer relationship management. A CRM tool provides an organized, comprehensive view of your company's customers and prospects, along with employees' interactions with them.

Once a large-business luxury, CRM software packages have come down in price and scale as they have migrated to hosted applications or web-based solutions, making CRM available to a growing number of small and mid-size businesses. Big players in the space include Salesforce and HubSpot; a number of providers, such as Insightly, offer free versions.

Regardless of which one your business chooses, CRM tools typically allow you to do the following:

- **Realize which customers produce the most profit.** By analyzing buying behaviors and other customer data, your business can gain a better understanding of who are your best customers. You can differentiate between the customer who provides the highest profit margins and those who simply bring you the most revenue.

- **Analyze buying patterns.** More understanding of customer buying patterns can help you spot potential high-value customers so that you can make the most of your sales opportunities with those customers.

- **Maximize per-customer profits.** Data gleaned from CRM can help you lower the cost of selling to certain customers and help you increase profits from those customer interactions.

---

4. **Make it a point to surround yourself with smart people.** There's a reason why the expression "If you're the smartest person in the room, you're in the wrong room" exists. It can be especially true when talking about trends and making sure your company evolves with them. An easy way to connect with informed people—and to keep your pulse on where things are heading—is to attend industry conferences. And consider going to an event or conference in an industry outside of your own, as a way to detect opportunities on the periphery of your business.

5. **Build and maintain a close group of advisors.** Depending on your company, you may already have a board of advisors that can provide input. You might also rely on a more informal group, such as friends, peers, and partners. Either way, find mentors or advisors who can show you different perspectives, help you see things that aren't on your radar, and—most important—spot what's coming around the corner.

6. **Ask the right questions, and listen to your customers.** Don't be afraid to ask current customers what's on their radars and what they see as future needs in their areas. You

can get solid insight into trends in general, and you can start developing more specific plans for your company to grow and better service clients down the road. "I love grabbing dinner with a current client, hearing more about what the next five years might look like for them, and finding out what they need from us along the way," Hall says.

7. **Learn to accept—and even embrace—change.** We get it—it's hard to try something different when you're in your comfort zone and things are going well for you. However, "if you get too comfortable and adapt to trends too late in the game, a competitor will beat you to the punch," Hall says. "Then, instead of staying ahead of those trends, you'll quickly try to play catch-up, which can cause even more problems in your execution." Accepting trends as facts of business can help you avoid that.

Starbucks

AS TOLD BY HOWARD Schultz, executive chairman of Starbucks:

Great entrepreneurs must have the curiosity to metaphorically see around the corner: What's coming, what can I anticipate that other people don't see. Then, you must have the courage of your convictions to execute the strategy.

The instant coffee category is a $24 billion category globally. It has not had any innovation for over fifty years. And it's dominated by one company. But for a company like Starbucks, whose image is based on high-quality, specialty coffee, to go into the instant coffee category, one could assume it would be a death sentence. When we announced we were doing this (introducing VIA), the media and Wall Street basically wanted to destroy me. The headlines were terrible. But again, I felt like we saw something that other people didn't see.

But the litmus test for this was that we had to replicate the taste of Starbucks coffee in an instant form. Once we cracked the code with technology, I knew right away that this would be a success. VIA has been a runaway hit for the company. This again was an opportunity to rekindle and remind the organization about the entrepreneurial spirit and the courage of the company to take the road less traveled. I don't believe there was any coffee company that could have done this other than us.

—

HOW STEVE JOBS DID IT

In 1989, the editors of *Inc.* announced that it took "about five minutes" to decide that the magazine's Entrepreneur of the Decade would be Steven P. Jobs, co-founder of Apple Computer Inc.

Inc. sat down with the famously private Jobs, who at that time had been forced out of Apple and was leading his new computer company, NeXT Inc. The magazine noted that Jobs, then thirty-three, had a reputation as brash, abrasive, and rough-edged. "But he also had dreams, big dreams, and the peculiar ability to develop products that seemed to give us a glimpse of a bright and exciting future," the editors wrote.

Q *INC.: Where do great products come from?*

A *JOBS:* I think really great products come from melding two points of view—the technology point of view and the customer point of view. You need both. You can't just ask customers what they want and then try to give that to them. By the time you get it built, they'll want something new. It took us three years to build the NeXT computer. If we'd given customers what they said they wanted, we'd have built a computer they'd have been happy with a year after we spoke to them—not something they'd want now.

Q *INC.: You mean the technology is changing too fast.*

A *JOBS:* Yeah, and customers can't anticipate what the technology can do. They won't ask for things that they think are impossible. But the technology may be ahead of them. If you happen to mention something, they'll say, "Of course, I'll take that. Do you mean I can have that, too?" It sounds logical to ask customers what they want and then give it to them. But they rarely wind up getting what they really want that way.

 INC.: It's got to be equally dangerous to focus too much on the technology.

JOBS: Oh, sure. You can get into just as much trouble by going into the technology lab and asking your engineers, "OK, what can you do for me today?" That rarely leads to a product that customers want or to one that you're very proud of building when you get done. You have to merge these points of view, and you have to do it in an interactive way over a period of time—which doesn't mean a week. It takes a long time to pull out of customers what they really want, and it takes a long time to pull out of technology what it can really give.

[In 1989, Jobs was working on machines that combined hardware and software in ways that had not been done before. His next comments presage the rise of the personal computer and ultimately the iPhone.]

INC.: What's so exciting about a souped-up microcomputer?

JOBS: I think humans are basically tool builders, and the

computer is the most remarkable tool we've ever built. The big insight a lot of us had in the 1970s had to do with the importance of putting that tool in the hands of individuals. Let's say that—for the same amount of money it takes to build the most powerful computer in the world—you could make a thousand computers with one-thousandth the power and put them in the hands of a thousand creative people. You'll get more out of doing that than out of having one person use the most powerful computer in the world. Because people are inherently creative. They will use tools in ways the toolmakers never thought possible. And once a person figures out how to do something with that tool, he or she can share it with the other 999.

INC.: That's a big idea.

JOBS: I believe this is one of the most important things that's going to happen in our generation. It would be easy to step back and say, "Well, it's pretty much over now." But if you look carefully, it's not over by any stretch of the imagination. The technological advances are coming at a rate that is far more ferocious than ever. To me, it's staggering to contemplate the tools we're going to be able to put in people's hands in the next few years—and I don't get impressed by this stuff so easily anymore.

For every improvement we can make in the tools we give people, we can improve the ultimate results even more. That's what gets us so excited.

INNOVATION 101:
THE IMPORTANCE OF CONSTANTLY DEVELOPING NEW PRODUCTS

The pursuit of startup success is what drives most entrepreneurs to innovate. Lean methodology (as discussed in Chapter 2) places a premium on testing, failing fast, pivoting, and finding clever, creative ways to stand out in a crowded marketplace.

Startups are in innovation mode because they're looking for a business model that works so they can scale. But unfortunately, "once established companies get a taste for success, the focus that once drove employees to search for the most innovative solution can shift to delivering the same, repeatable solution over and over again," says Jeff Pruitt, founder of Tallwave, a strategic consulting firm.

It's understandable that innovation can slow as a company grows up. Once you've got something that works, it's difficult to change course. It's also a natural human reaction to success—if you worked hard to achieve it, you likely want to safeguard it at all costs.

But what happens when your product or service stops drawing a crowd and customers start looking elsewhere for flashier—yet similar—solutions?

"B2B companies are especially hesitant to innovate once a successful model is found," Pruitt says. And consumer product companies, so vulnerable to consumers' changing tastes, can drag their feet when it comes to investing in new product development. No company can exist in the same form forever, however, and in today's fast-paced world, the road to obsolescence is shorter than ever.

Simply put, if you don't innovate, you can be sure your competitors will. Of course, figuring out the right ways to innovate within an already established brand framework is difficult. To properly innovate, you need to get back to the basics. "You know, the kind of thinking that got you to this point in the first place," Pruitt says. Here's how.

1. **Revisit the customer journey. Just on a much larger scale.** Treat your current product offerings like competition and work tirelessly to better them. You don't necessarily want to intentionally build short shelf lives into your products (which some critics say Apple does), but you do want to evolve your brand so that it transforms alongside your customer over the long haul.

   One company that does this is Salesforce, which pioneered something called the IdeaExchange—a platform that allows customers to interact with one another, communicate with the company, and suggest new features. "So many companies pay lip service to consumer feedback," says Pruitt. But "the best ones integrate feedback—after all, the best source for learning about the customer journey is the customers themselves."

2. **Incorporate innovation into your budget.** The last thing you want to do is innovate yourself into financial trouble. When you were in the startup phase this wasn't as much of a concern—you were always hyper-aware of your financial restraints. At this stage of your company, it's wise

to seek out partners or advisors who can understand the capital expenses of expansion and help you maximize your return.

It can be difficult to invest in the long term, however, when you're more focused in the short term on making payroll and staying profitable. (Young public companies, for instance, often stop innovating once the VCs that pushed for new ideas are replaced by shareholders who want steady, stable growth in the short term.) "You need to incorporate an innovation strategy into your budget and put internal teams together whose primary focus is keeping a mind on what's next," Pruitt advises.

Google, for instance, budgets 20 percent of its employees' time for brainstorming on outside projects. Side note: If you fear losing touch with customers, look to your own employees for inspiration first.

3. **Keep the focus on your next great product.** Established brands are more prone to nervous decision making when a new competitor pops up in their space. That's why we often see clunky, rushed "innovations" in the form of an app no one wants or a rebranding campaign that doesn't speak to the right audience.

The solution: Stop focusing on your last great idea and start thinking about your next one.

One company that has successfully kept the focus on new innovation is Square. In 2009, it was first out of the gates in the mobile payment game, changing transactions with a simple idea (and a dongle). When banks and other startups began rolling out early versions of mobile money transfers, Square responded. In 2013, it launched Cash, its own peer-to-peer payment app. The innovation "was proof that fans of Square wouldn't have to jump to a different platform to find a company that evolves with them," Pruitt says.

As a growing company, you might have to work twice as hard to rediscover your nimble roots. But if done correctly, your customers will stay along for the ride and you'll pick up a few more along the way.

Lego

THE GOOD NEWS IS, failures to anticipate marketplace changes aren't always fatal.

Danish toy maker Lego was on the verge of bankruptcy in 2003, after underestimating competition from video games and the Internet. So the beloved toy company, founded in 1932, changed its approach.

It invested in research, creating a top-secret R&D team called Future Lab to understand how kids around the world really play. It began keeping tabs on what the competition was up to. It improved communications with retailers and customers, viewing them as strategic radar and sources of new ideas.

Lego teamed up with outside inventors to create new products. Other outside parties helped it create T-shirts, movies, books, toys, and games. Lego also developed robotic kits to replace its 1998 product, emphasizing intelligent bricks, a new programming language, motors and sensors, starter models, and teaching materials for schools. In 2011, Lego launched a major initiative to attract girls to the brand, debuting a line called Lego Friends.

Lego rebounded from a vast deficit in 2004 to become the world's most profitable toymaker in 2014, with $4.5 billion in sales. It even managed to overtake Mattel, which makes a range of products (Barbie, Hot Wheels, Fisher-Price), while Lego mostly sticks to bricks.

But it would have been much better if the company anticipated the market changes before they nearly did it in.

—

DEBUNKING THE MYTH OF INNOVATION

"My idea must be a breakthrough."

Many people equate the idea of innovation with disruptive innovation. "But the fact is that for most businesses, placing big bets on high-risk ideas is not only unfeasible, it's unwise," says Adam Bluestein, a contributing writer at *Inc.*

On average, the most successful companies devote about 70 percent of their innovation assets (time and money) to "safe" core initiatives; 20 percent to slightly riskier adjacent ones; and just 10 percent to transformational, or disruptive, ones. That's according to a 2012 report by innovation consultants Bansi Nagji and Geoff Tuff.

Core innovation involves making incremental changes to improve existing products for existing customers—think selling laundry detergent in capsule form. Adjacent innovations draw on a company's existing capabilities and put them to new uses—see Procter & Gamble's Swiffer, a re-envisioning of the old-fashioned mop to attract a new set of customers. Transformational (a.k.a., disruptive) innovations involve inventing things for markets that don't exist yet—say, the automobile or the Internet.

The 70:20:10 ratio isn't set in stone. "Depending on your industry, your competitive position in it, and your stage of growth, you may need to make adjustments," Bluestein says. Tech companies, for example, tend to spend less time and money improving core products because their market craves novelty, and so they may put more effort into risky ideas. Consumer-products companies with established product lines tend to focus mostly on incremental innovations.

Of course, when a disruptive innovation succeeds, the returns can be enormous, with 70 percent of total returns coming from breakthrough initiatives. Bottom line: Every business needs some practice coming up with ideas that will change everything, but it is unwise to let the pursuit of the breakthrough overshadow the many smaller initiatives that sustain a business over the long run.

Here's a look at three more innovation misconceptions.

1. **"You can't have too many ideas."** Sure you can, if you don't know what to do with them.

   Coming up with ideas isn't nearly as hard as determining which ones are any good and figuring out what to do with them. Small companies can be crushed under the weight of too many ideas. When you're running a business, a big part of your job is to kill the weak ones.

   But most companies lack processes to decide which ideas to pursue, much less ways to measure their success. Picking the right ideas starts with being clear about your company's mission. A cool idea that excites your engineers should never become a working project until someone can articulate how it actually solves a pressing problem that your customers have. The business case for pursuing an innovation should include an indication of how to measure its impact, says Robert Sher, founding principal of the Bay Area consulting firm CEO to CEO. "The goal could be increasing brand awareness, customer satisfaction, customer retention," Sher says. "Make sure you measure something crucial to your outcome."

2. **"Innovation is about stuff."** It's not—and you might want to consider a business-model revamp instead.

Most companies focus most of their innovation efforts on new products and product extensions, according to research by the consultancy Doblin. But these kinds of innovations, it turns out, are the least likely to return their cost of investment, with a success rate of only 4.5 percent. Instead, Doblin found, companies get the highest return on investment when they focus on things such as improving business models, internal processes, and customer experience.

"The most valuable innovations are platform-level innovations," says Larry Keeley, a director at Deloitte and the author of *Ten Types of Innovation*. Though Apple is rightly famous for well-designed devices, he says, "Apple's most valuable innovation is the iTunes store." Almost as integral to Apple's success have been the company's aggressive tax-avoidance strategies—such as creating offices and subsidiaries in low-tax locales such as Nevada, Ireland, and the British Virgin Islands. "It's created a very advantaged business model," says Keeley.

Similarly, Amazon makes little money on Kindle sales. The device's real value comes from the way Amazon has linked it to its massive inventory of ebooks. Other examples of non-product innovation include the collaborative-consumption models of Zipcar or Airbnb, Zappos's positioning of itself as "a service company that just happens to sell shoes," and the values-driven strategies of Patagonia and Whole Foods.

Rather than obsessing over your next new product or service, it might be smarter to work on a new profit model or a better customer experience.

3. **"Innovation is costly."** Actually, spending has little to do with results. Apple, ranked as the most innovative company for the past three years, spends just 2.2 percent of its sales on R&D efforts. That's well below the industry average of 6.5 percent for computing and electronics and far less than rivals such as Google, Samsung, and Microsoft. In fact, Apple ranks fifty-third among the 1,000 top R&D spenders in all industries.

   "There's a logic fallacy that if you spend more, you get more innovation," says Michael Schrage, a research fellow at MIT and an advisor on innovation to companies such as Procter & Gamble and Herman Miller. Measuring innovation properly, Schrage says, means getting away from looking at inputs—that is, your R&D dollars—and focusing on the outputs that your efforts are generating with customers. "Unless you can show that customers and clients are getting more value from your new offerings," Schrage says, "it's less likely to be innovation and more likely to be waste."

Box

THE DIFFERENCE BETWEEN LARGE companies and large innovative companies might come down to how they listen to their customers, says Aaron Levie, co-founder and CEO of Box. Founded in 2005, the file-sharing and content-management company in April 2017 had more than 71,000 enterprise customers (and was *Inc.*'s 2013 Company of the Year). But size is more albatross than advantage when it comes to innovation.

"When we had a couple hundred customers, it wasn't a big enough base to tell us where they wanted to go, so we made big bets," Levie says. "The bigger you get, the bigger the instinct to listen to what customers want and to think customers have all the answers."

This can lead to incremental improvements on existing products, but few big, exciting innovations, he says. To keep Box ahead, Levie regularly checks in with a small subset of a few hundred forward-thinking customers. That focus group has helped the Redwood City, California, company set itself apart in the crowded file-sharing space. Its governance and compliance offerings, especially, allow heavily regulated industries like health care and financial services to embrace the cloud. And a limited customer focus is driving Levie to pursue what he thinks all customers will come to expect in the future: machine learning. Box is now developing artificial intelligence solutions to help customers get more insights from their data.

"We have a very fast feedback loop with that small set of customers," says Levie. "And as they adopt the next innovation, it will ripple through the customer base."

—

BECOME AN EXCEPTIONAL LEADER

" Fortune does favor the bold and you'll never know what you're capable of if you don't try."

—

SHERYL SANDBERG, chief operating officer of Facebook.

A TOUGH THING ABOUT LAUNCHING a new business is that you typically need to do everything yourself—especially in the early days, before you have staff.

But then something even more challenging happens as you grow, hire, and expand. When you've got employees, customers, suppliers, and partners depending on you, then you need to become a leader.

Which gets us to an important questions: Are great leaders born or made?

We've asked a number of experts this very same question. The consensus: Leadership is a learned skill. Sure, there are inborn characteristics that can predispose some people to be leaders. But anyone with persistence, discipline, and passion can develop the abilities necessary to lead—and to do so exceptionally.

So that gets us to another important question: What makes a leader great?

Leadership is a difficult thing to pin down and understand. You know a great leader when you're around one, but even great leaders can have a hard time explaining the specifics of what they do that makes their leadership so effective.

Over the years, we've interviewed countless successful entrepreneurs, and we've identified five traits or attributes that most share. From this, we've concluded that to be an exceptional leader, you need to do the following:

→ Be decisive

→ Communicate effectively

→ Behave generously

→ Learn self-awareness

→ Exude charisma

In the pages ahead, we'll take a look at each trait, and provide some practical advice on how to get better at some aspects of leadership. The more you practice, the more instinctive it will become, and the more you'll internalize your new leadership style.

TRAIT #1
DECISIVENESS

All leaders must make courageous decisions. It goes with the job. You understand that in certain situations, some difficult and timely decisions must be made in the best interests of the entire organization. Such decisions require a firmness, authority, and finality that will not please everyone.

ADVICE:
HOW TO BE DECISIVE

❝❝ I think everybody who creates something is doing something audacious. Because the most difficult time is when you are starting from scratch with no financial backing—just an idea. So true audaciousness comes about with just those people who have the pluck and the courage to say, 'Screw it; let's do it.'"

—

RICHARD BRANSON, Virgin Group chairman

There are a few truths when it comes to decision making, according to Anna Johansson, a business consultant:

→ **Logical decisions tend to trump emotional ones.** Since emotions can sometimes make us biased or see things in an inaccurate light, basing a decision on logic, rather than on a current emotional state, usually gives you more objective information to make the final call.

→ **Thought-out decisions tend to trump impulsive ones.** Because you've spent more time on the problem, you'll understand it more thoroughly and be better versed in the variables that might arise from any possible route.

→ **Flexible decisions tend to trump concrete ones.** Things change frequently, so making a decision that allows for some eventual degree of flexibility usually offers more adaptable options than a decision that's absolute or concrete.

These aren't absolute rules, however. For example, many entrepreneurs trust their gut when making decisions—and indeed, instinct can sometimes beat over-analytical thinking.

Here are some strategies you can use in almost any decision-making process to ensure that you make the best choice, according to Johansson:

Step Away From the Problem

Scientific research suggests that distancing yourself from a problem can help you face it in a more objective way. For example, let's say you're trying to choose between two different opportunities, and you can't tell which one is better for you. Instead of remaining in your own frame of mind, consider yourself as an outside observer, such as a mentor giving advice or a fly on the wall. Removing yourself in this way helps you filter out some of your cognitive biases and lean you toward a more rational decision.

Give Yourself Some Time

Most of us end up being lousy decision makers when we try to force a decision in a moment, or push through to a final choice after first learning about a situation. In some high-pressure environments, this is a must, but it isn't the most effective or rewarding way to do things. Instead, accuracy and reliability in decision making tends to increase if you first give yourself some time to decompress and collect yourself—even if it's just a few minutes. This may also help you remove yourself from the problem, knocking out two of these strategies in one fell swoop.

Know That There Is No Right Answer

You can stress yourself out trying to pin down the answer that's objectively correct, if you believe one such answer exists. Instead, remind yourself that there's almost never an objectively correct answer. "All you can do is make the decision that's the best for you at the time, and it's probably going to work out okay either way," Johansson says.

Forget the Past

Remember the lessons you've learned from the past, but don't let your past experiences affect what you choose in the present. For example, if you've paid a hundred dollars a month for a service that isn't getting you anywhere, you may be tempted to continue simply for the reason that you've already spent thousands of dollars. This skewed line of reasoning is an example of an escalation bias, in which you're hesitant to cut your losses. You can't change the past, so instead, look to the present and future.

Commit

You can overanalyze a problem as much as you like, but it probably isn't going to help anything. It's just going to bring up new complications, force you to second-guess yourself, and possibly double back on a decision you've already made. All of these will make the process more excruciating and will make you unsatisfied with whatever decision you land on. Instead, pick an option early and fully commit to it.

There's no perfect way to make a decision, and there are very few situations in which a decision is ever "right." However, with these strategies in tow, you'll be well-equipped to make more rational, complete, and best of all, satisfying decisions in your life.

TRAIT #2:
EFFECTIVE COMMUNICATION

Communication is the real work of leadership. It's a fundamental element of how leaders accomplish goals each and every day. You simply can't become a great leader until you are a great communicator.

Great communicators inspire people. They forge a connection with their followers that is real, emotional, and personal, regardless of any physical distance between them. Great communicators tell stories and paint verbal pictures so that everyone can understand not just where they're going but what it will look and feel like when they get there. This inspires others to internalize the vision and make it their own.

ADVICE:
HOW TO BE A BETTER COMMUNICATOR

“ Today, we're introducing three revolutionary products....the first one is a widescreen iPod with touch controls. The second is a revolutionary mobile phone. And the third is a breakthrough Internet communications device. So, three things: a widescreen iPod with touch controls; a revolutionary mobile phone; and a breakthrough Internet communications device. An iPod, a phone, and an Internet communicator. An iPod, a phone.... Are you getting it? These are not three separate devices, this is one device, and we are calling it iPhone.”

—
STEVE JOBS INTRODUCING THE IPHONE IN 2007

Communication skills are a powerful tool to have in your arsenal. Here are eight proven strategies that will improve yours, according to Travis Bradberry, coauthor of *Emotional Intelligence 2.0*.

Speak to Groups as Individuals

As a leader, you often have to speak to groups of people. Whether a small team meeting or a companywide gathering, you need to develop a level of intimacy in your approach that makes each individual in the room feel as if you're speaking directly to him or her. The trick is to eliminate the distraction of the crowd so that you can deliver your message just as you would if you were talking to a single person. You want to be emotionally genuine and exude the same feelings, energy, and attention you would one-on-one (as opposed to the anxiety that comes with being in front of people). "The ability to pull this off is the hallmark of great leadership communication," Bradberry says.

Talk So People Will Listen

Great communicators read their audience (groups and individuals) carefully to ensure they aren't wasting their breath on a message that people aren't ready to hear. Talking so people will listen means you adjust your message on the fly to stay with your audience (what they're ready to hear and how they're ready to hear it). Droning on to ensure you've said what you wanted to say does not have the same effect on people as engaging them in a meaningful dialogue in which there is an exchange of ideas. Resist the urge to drive your point home at all costs. When your talking leads to people asking good questions, you know you're on the right track.

Listen So People Will Talk

One of the most disastrous temptations for a leader is to treat communication as a one-way street. When you communicate, you must give people ample opportunity to speak their minds. If you find that you're often having the last word in conversations, then this is likely something you need to work on.

Listening isn't just about hearing words; it's also about listening to the tone, speed, and volume of the voice. What is being said? Anything not being said? What hidden messages exist below the surface? When someone is talking to you, stop everything else and listen fully until the other person has finished speaking, Bradberry advises. When you are on a phone call, don't type an email. When you're meeting with someone, close the door and sit near the person so you can focus and listen. Simple behaviors like these will help you stay in the present moment, pick up on the cues the other person sends, and make it clear that you will really hear what he or she is saying.

Connect Emotionally

Maya Angelou said it best: "People will forget what you said and did, but they will never forget how you made them feel." As a leader, your communication is impotent if people don't connect with it on an emotional level. This is hard for many leaders to pull off because they feel they need to project a certain persona. Let that go. To connect with your people emotionally, you need to be transparent. Be human. Show them what drives you, what you care about, what makes you get out of bed in the morning. Express these feelings openly, and you'll forge an emotional connection with your team.

Read Body Language

Your authority makes it hard for people to say what's really on their minds. "No matter how good a relationship you have with your subordinates, you are kidding yourself if you think they are as open with you as they are with their peers," Bradberry says. So, you must become adept at understanding unspoken messages. The greatest wealth of information lies in people's body language. The body communicates nonstop and is an abundant source of information, so purposefully watch body language during meetings and casual conversation. Once you tune into body language, the messages will become loud and clear. Pay as much attention to what isn't said as what is said, and you'll uncover facts and opinions that people are unwilling to express directly. (For more, see "Common Body Language Mistakes," page 184.)

Prepare Your Intent

A little preparation goes a long way toward saying what you wanted to say and having a conversation achieve its intended impact. Don't prepare a speech; develop an understanding of what the focus of a conversation needs to be (in order for people to hear the message) and how you will accomplish this. Your communication will be more persuasive and on point when you prepare your intent ahead of time.

Skip the Jargon

The business world is filled with jargon and metaphors that are harmless when people can relate to them. Problem is, most leaders overuse jargon and alienate their subordinates and customers with their "business speak." Use it sparingly if you want to connect with people. Otherwise, you'll come across as insincere.

Practice Active Listening

Active listening is a simple technique that ensures people feel heard, an essential component of good communication, according to Bradberry. To practice active listening, he recommends doing the following:

→ Spend more time listening than you do talking.

→ Do not answer questions with questions.

→ Avoid finishing other people's sentences.

→ Focus more on the other person than you do on yourself.

→ Focus on what people are saying right now, not on what their interests are.

→ Reframe what the other person has said to make sure you understand him or her correctly ("So you're telling me that this budget needs further consideration, right?")

→ Think about what you're going to say after someone has finished speaking, not while he or she is speaking.

→ Ask plenty of questions.

→ Never interrupt.

→ Don't take notes.

As you work to employ these eight strategies, try to avoid biting off more than you can chew. "Working on one to three strategies at a time is sufficient," Bradberry says. "If you try to take on more than you can handle, you're not going to see as much progress as you would if you narrowed your focus." Once you become effective in one particular strategy, you can take on another one in its place.

Communication is a dynamic element of leadership that is intertwined in most of what you do each day. You'll have ample opportunity to improve your abilities in this critical skill.

Common Body Language Mistakes

The brain picks up nonverbal cues in a fifth of a second, much faster than verbal ones, according to Minda Zeltin, an Inc.com columnist and coauthor of *The Geek Gap*. "Don't let your unconscious signals send the wrong message," she says. "Learn to avoid these all-too-easy mistakes."

1. **Leaning back.** If you want to signal that you care about a conversation or the person you're having it with, don't lean back and stick your legs out in front of you. Sit up straight, or lean in.

2. **Crossed arms and/or legs.** This is such a clear indicator of lack of interest that some experts recommend actually ending a meeting or conversation if you see one or more people lean back and cross their arms. Crossed legs may be a danger sign as well.

3. Not making eye contact. If you don't look the person in front of you in the eyes, he or she may unconsciously assume that you are being dishonest. Practiced liars make a point of looking in people's eyes—so don't make the mistake of equating eye contact with honesty yourself.

4. Making too much eye contact. Not looking someone in the eyes can make you seem dishonest, but looking them in the eyes for too long is usually a sign of aggression. To make people feel comfortable and trusting, hold their gaze for just a second or two at a time, but do it often.

5. Clasped hands. This is something people do when they feel stress—you're literally holding your own hand! Don't do it if you want to project self-assurance.

6. Hands behind back or in pockets. This is a natural position many of us take unconsciously, but it can be seen as a sign that we have something to hide.

7. Chopping the air. Many people do this when they feel strongly about something or want to emphasize a point. But it can be off-putting—almost as if you're chopping off your connection with the person you're speaking with.

8. Touching your face. Touching your face, especially your nose and mouth, is another one of those gestures that is unconsciously interpreted as a sign of deception—or resistance, if you're listening rather than speaking.

9. **Nodding too many times.** Nodding is an essential part of communication and lets other people know you understand or agree with what they're saying. But doing it too many times can make you seem weak. It can also come across as a sign of indifference.

10. **Fidgeting.** People fidget when they're uncomfortable or bored, so that's the signal you'll send if you're bouncing your leg or constantly messing with your hair. Just don't do it.

11. **Hunching your shoulders.** Hunched or slumped shoulders are seen as a sign of unhappiness—and they often are. To project happiness and confidence, stand up straight, like mom nagged you to do.

12. **Wrapping your feet or ankles around the legs of a chair.** Like clasped hands, this gesture signals that you're uncomfortable and need to comfort yourself. If you're trying to project confidence, don't do it.

13. **Making yourself too small.** Social psychologist Amy Cuddy's fascinating research on nonverbal behavior shows that people who practice expansive body language feel more confident or secure as a result. The reverse is also true: Body language that makes you seem small will make you feel small.

14. **Overly big gestures.** Your body language should be expansive to project confidence. But don't make the mistake of making great big gestures (unless you're on

stage speaking to an audience). In a non-performance context, it can be seen as arrogant.

15. **Letting your feet point the wrong way.** Our feet often unconsciously express what we're really feeling, for example by pointing away from the person we're speaking with. Most people pay more attention to faces, but it's a good idea to keep your feet on-message as well.

16. **Patting your leg or legs.** This is a huge self-comforting gesture that will show how uncomfortable you are. Watch Britney Spears on *Dateline* gamely claiming her marriage was fine a few months before her divorce. She can't stop touching her leg.

17. **Glancing at a watch or phone.** We think we can peek at the time or a text without people noticing, but they always do. Don't shift your attention from the conversation unless you absolutely have to. If so, explain why—that you are awaiting an urgent message, for example.

18. **Touching someone with your fingertips.** In appropriate situations, touching someone lightly is a great way to begin building a bond (or to indicate romantic interest). But use your whole hand. A fingertip touch signals aversion.

19. **Failing to "mirror."** People who are listening closely to what someone else is saying will often unconsciously mirror that person's body language. Use this technique—consciously or unconsciously—to let people know you really care about what they have to say.

20. Invading someone's personal space. We all have a different idea of how much buffer we need around ourselves to feel comfortable. So when you come close to someone, err on the side of giving that person a little extra room.

21. Forgetting that these rules might be different in different places. Body language has very different meanings in other cultures. Keep that in mind when dealing with people from different countries, or even other parts of this country.

" You know, as most entrepreneurs do, that a company is only as good as its people. The hard part is actually building the team that will embody your company's culture and propel you forward."

—

KATHRYN MINSHEW, co-founder of career-advice site The Muse

TRAIT #3:
GENEROSITY

If you want to lead exceptionally, then you need to be generous, sharing credit and offering enthusiastic praise. You should be as committed to your followers' success as you are to your own. Great leaders want to inspire all of their employees to achieve their personal best—not just because it will make the team more successful, but also because they care about each person as an individual.

ADVICE:
HOW TO PRAISE EMPLOYEES, THE RIGHT WAY

Praise can be incredibly motivating. Praise can be extremely encouraging. Praise can be hugely inspiring—if you do it the right way. Take the wrong approach, and praising an employee can actually have the opposite effect.

The difference lies in whether you assume skill is based on innate ability...or on hard work and effort. "Put another way, are people simply born with special talent, or can incredible talent be developed?" asks Jeff Haden, an Inc.com columnist. "I think talent can definitely be developed, and so should you."

According to research on achievement and success by Stanford psychologist Carol Dweck, people tend to embrace one of two mental approaches to talent:

→ **Fixed mindset.** The belief that intelligence, ability, and skill are inborn and relatively immovable—we have what we were born with. People with a fixed mindset typically say things like, "I'm just not that smart" or "Math is not my thing."

→ **Growth mindset.** The belief that intelligence, ability, and skill can be developed through effort—we are what we work to become. People with a growth mindset typically say things like, "With a little more time, I'll get it" or "That's OK. I'll give it another try."

That difference in perspective can be molded by the kind of praise we receive, and that often starts when we're children. For example, say a young person is praised in one of these ways:

→ "Wow, you figured that out so quickly—you are so smart!"

→ "Wow, you are amazing—you got an A without even cracking a book!"

Sounds great, right? The problem is that other messages are lurking within those statements:

→ "If I ever *don't* figure things out quickly...then I must not be very smart."

→ "If I *do* ever have to study...then I must not be amazing."

The result can be that the person adopts a fixed mindset: He assumes he is what he is. Then, when the going gets tough...he struggles and feels helpless because he thinks what he "is" isn't good enough. And when he thinks he isn't good enough—and never will be—he stops trying.

When you praise employees only for their achievements—or criticize employees for their short-term failures—you help create a fixed mindset environment, according to Haden. "In time, employees come to see every mistake as a failure," he says. "They see a lack of immediate results as failure. In time, they can lose motivation—and even stop trying."

Fortunately, there's another way, Haden says. Make sure you also praise effort and application.

→ "Hey, you finished that project much more quickly this time. You must have worked really hard."

→ "Great job! I can tell you put a lot of time into that."

→ "That didn't go as well as we hoped...but all the work you put in is definitely paying off. Let's see what we can do to make things turn out even better next time."

That way you still praise (or critique) results—but you praise results that are based on the premise of effort, not on an assumption of innate talent or skill. By praising effort, you help create an environment where employees feel anything is possible—as long as they keep working to improve.

The same principle applies to how you encourage employees. Don't say, "You're really smart. I know you'll get this." While that sounds complimentary (and it is), "You're really smart" assumes an innate quality the employee either has or does not have.

Instead, say, "I have faith in you. You're a hard worker. I've never seen you give up. I know you'll get this."

The best way to consistently improve employee performance is to create and foster a growth mindset. Not only will your team's skills improve, your employees will also be more willing to take more risks.

When failure is seen as just a step on the road to eventual achievement, risks are no longer something to avoid. Risk, and occasional failure, will simply be an expected step on the way to inevitable success.

TRAIT #4:
SELF-AWARENESS

" When you first come into a position where you are in leadership, and you have a lot of employees underneath you, odds are you're not going to know everything. You're not going to have all the answers. And you're not going to come across as completely polished and knowing it all. Rather than trying to trick people into thinking that you have all the answers, just be upfront and straight from the beginning. Admit your weaknesses. Admit your faults. Because if you do that, then you're going to earn their trust."

—

CRISTINA MARIANI-MAY, co-CEO of Banfi Wines, a family-owned wine importer with $300 million in revenue

Self-awareness is the foundation of emotional intelligence, a skill that most top performing leaders possess in abundance. Great leaders' high self-awareness means they have a clear and accurate image not just of their leadership style but also of their strengths and weaknesses. They know where they shine and where they're weak, and they have effective strategies for leaning into their strengths and compensating for their weaknesses.

ADVICE:
HOW TO BOOST YOUR
EMOTIONAL INTELLIGENCE

In 1995, psychologist Daniel Goleman published the best-selling book *Emotional Intelligence*, discounting IQ as the sole measure of one's abilities. His research on business leadership, published in 1998 in the *Harvard Business Review*, found that emotional intelligence sets star performers apart from the rest of the pack. Goleman likened IQ and technical skills to entry-level requirements for executive positions, noting that emotional intelligence is necessary for leadership.

"Emotional intelligence is the 'something' in each of us that is a bit intangible," says Travis Bradberry, co-founder of TalentSmart, a San Diego provider of emotional intelligence tests. "It affects how we manage behavior, navigate social complexities, and make personal decisions that achieve positive results."

Emotional intelligence taps into a fundamental element of human behavior that is distinct from your intellect. There is no known connection between IQ and emotional intelligence; you simply can't predict emotional intelligence based on how smart someone is, Bradberry says. Intelligence is your ability to learn, and it's the same at age fifteen as it is at age fifty.

Emotional intelligence, on the other hand, is a flexible set of skills that can be acquired and improved with practice. Although some people are naturally more emotionally intelligent than others, you can develop high emotional intelligence even if you aren't born with it.

How much of an impact does emotional intelligence have on your professional success? "The short answer is: A lot," says Bradberry. "It's a powerful way to focus your energy in one direction with a tremendous result." Bradberry's firm says it tested emotional intelligence alongside thirty-three other workplace skills, and found that emotional intelligence is the strongest predictor of performance, explaining a full 58 percent of success in all types of jobs.

So how do you develop emotional intelligence? As with any skill, it takes some study and practice.

Justin Bariso, author of *EQ, Applied,* offers this series of practical steps that can help you increase your EQ:

Reflect on Your Own Emotions

Take some time to sit down and reflect on your own use of emotions. For example, think about how you typically respond when:

→ You read an email that implies you dropped the ball

→ Your significant other blames you for something you feel is unfair

→ Another driver cuts you off on the highway

→ A close friend or associate begins to cry unexpectedly

By first identifying your own emotions and reactions, you become more mindful and start the process of building control.

Ask Others for Perspective

Often, we don't realize that other people view us much differently than we view ourselves, and vice versa. It's not about right or wrong; it's simply understanding how perceptions differ, and the consequences those differences create.

By asking those close to us—like a significant other, close friend, or workmate—about our interactions with them, we can learn from their perspective. For example, we could think about a specific time when we were in a highly emotional state. Ask the other person: Did I act out of the ordinary during that time? Could you describe how?

Then, ask them to relate experiences regarding when they were going through an emotional situation.

You can ask:

→ How did I deal with you at that time?

→ Would you say I was sensitive to your feelings and emotions?

Getting the answers to these questions will help us to see ourselves more like others see us—and help us to understand others better, too. You can then use that knowledge to adjust your dealings with others.

Be Observant

Armed with this newly acquired knowledge, you can now be more observant of your current emotions. Your self-reflection and what others have shared will help you to be more in tune with what you're feeling.

If you make any new discoveries, make sure to repeat step one. You can even write down your experience; doing so will help clarify your thinking and keep you in "learning mode."

Use "The Pause"

"The pause" may be as simple as taking a moment to stop and think before we act or speak. If everyone made that a practice, imagine how much shorter emails could be, how much time would be saved in meetings, and how many incendiary comments on social media would be eliminated.

But remember: The pause is easy in theory, difficult to practice.

Even if we're generally good at managing our emotions, factors like added stress or a bad day can inhibit our ability to do so at any given time. And we're not just talking about upsetting situations; we are often tempted to jump on opportunities that look really good at the time but that we haven't really thought through.

When you work on pausing before speaking or acting, you create a habit of thinking first.

Explore the "Why"

Most of us would agree that qualities like empathy and compassion are valuable ingredients to healthy relationships. So, why do we often neglect to show those qualities when it matters most—like when we fail to show understanding to a close friend or partner when they're going through a difficult time?

Scientists have studied what psychologist and author Adam Grant calls "the perspective gap." In short, this term describes the fact that it's extremely challenging to put ourselves in another person's shoes. We often forget how specific situations feel, even if we've experienced very similar circumstances. (If we've never experienced something similar, you can imagine how that limits our perspective.)

So, how do we bridge the gap?

Demonstrating qualities such as empathy and compassion means that we try our best to see a situation through another person's eyes. But we have to go further than drawing on our own experiences; showing true empathy means exploring the why:

→ Why does this person feel the way she does?

→ What is she dealing with that I don't see?

→ Why do I feel differently than she does?

If you can't effectively answer those questions, consider working alongside the person for a period of time to truly understand what's going on, as viewed from that person's perspective. Doing so will help you see your team and family members not as complainers, but for who they really are: Struggling individuals who need help.

When Criticized, Don't Take Offense. Instead, Ask: What Can I Learn?

As an entrepreneur, criticism is never easy to take. You've invested blood, sweat, and sometimes tears in your work. It can be extremely difficult when someone else comes in and knocks down what you've built.

But the truth is, criticism is often rooted in truth—even when it's not delivered in an ideal manner. When you receive negative feedback, there are two choices: You can put your feelings aside and try to learn from the situation, or you can get angry and let emotion get the best of you.

When we are on the receiving end of criticism, whether it's delivered ideally or not, it's invaluable to consider the following:

→ Putting my personal feelings aside, what can I learn from this alternate perspective?

→ Instead of focusing on the delivery, how can I use this feedback to help me or my team improve?

There are times when you shouldn't listen to criticism—for example, when it's based on falsehood or given in a way that's meant to destroy your sense of self-worth. But that's not usually the case. If your goal is to truly get better, don't let emotion close your mind to negative feedback. Instead, learn from it.

Practice, Practice, Practice

Like any other skill or ability, practice makes...

Better. Of course, it's impossible to have perfect control over your emotions. And learning to improve your emotional intelligence isn't a process that happens overnight.

However, consistently practicing these steps will allow you to begin harnessing the power of emotions—and to use that power to work for you, instead of against you.

TRAIT #5:
CHARISMA

Charismatic leaders believe in something powerfully and share that belief with others. Their conviction and consistent actions influence others to follow. Dedicated followers add exponentially to the energy that radiates from a charismatic leader.

If you want to be charismatic, you need to connect empathetically. Charismatic people make you laugh, they make you feel heard, they make you feel special or fascinated or safe or interesting.

ADVICE:
HOW TO BE MORE CHARISMATIC

Some people instantly make us feel important. Some people instantly make us feel special. Some people light up a room just by walking in.

We can't always define it, but some people have it: They're charismatic.

People who have charisma build and maintain great relationships, and consistently influence—in a positive way—the people around them. They're the kind of people everyone wants to be around...and wants to be. "Fortunately we can, because being remarkably charismatic isn't about our level of success or our presentation skills or how we dress or the image we project," says Inc.com columnist Jeff Haden. "It's about what we do."

Here are ten habits of charismatic people, which anybody can practice:

Listen More Than You Talk

Ask questions. Maintain eye contact. Smile. Frown. Nod. Respond—not so much verbally, but nonverbally. That's all it takes to show other people that they're important.

When you do speak, don't offer advice unless you're asked. "Listening shows you care a lot more than offering advice," Haden says. Most people who are quick to offer advice say, "Here's what I would do...," effectively making the conversation about them.

Don't Practice Selective Hearing

Some people hear only what serves their interests. They often don't listen if they feel that the person doing the talking is beneath them in some capacity.

Charismatic people, in contrast, listen closely to everyone, and they make everyone, regardless of position or social status or level, feel like they have something in common with the listener. "Which they do—we're all people, after all," Haden says.

> **❝** I think of myself as an entrepreneur, but I love investing. People allow me to invest in their dreams, and I don't have to come up with everything myself. They're doing business in a whole new way and I'm fortunate enough to be partnering with them."
>
> —
> **DAYMOND JOHN,** Fubu founder and *Shark Tank* star

Put Your Stuff Away

In today's highly connected the world, give someone the gift of your full attention. Don't check your phone. Don't glance at your monitor. Don't focus on anything else, even for a moment. You can never connect with others if you're busy connecting with your devices, too.

Give Before You Receive—Even if You Never Receive

Never think about what you can get. Focus on what you can provide. Giving is the only way to establish a real connection and relationship. When you focus on what you can get out of another person, "you show that the only person who really matters is you," Haden says.

Don't Act Self-important...

Generally speaking, the only people who are impressed by stuffy, pretentious, self-important types are other stuffy, pretentious, self-important types. Most people are irritated, put off, and uncomfortable.

...Instead, Recognize That Other People Are More Important

You already know your own opinions, perspectives, and points of view. "But you don't know what other people know, and everyone, no matter who they are, knows things you don't know," Haden says. "That makes them a lot more important—they're people you can learn from."

Shine the Spotlight on Others

Not only will people appreciate your praise, they'll appreciate the fact you care enough to pay attention to what they're doing. Then they'll feel a little more accomplished and a lot more important.

Choose Your Words

The words you use can impact the attitude of others. For example, you don't "have to interview job candidates"; you get to "select a great person to join your team." You don't "have to create a presentation"; you get to "share cool stuff with a new client." You don't "have to go to the gym"; you get to "work out and improve your health and fitness." We all want to associate with happy, enthusiastic, fulfilled people. The words you choose can help other people feel better about themselves—and make you feel better about yourself, too.

Don't Discuss the Failings of Others...

Granted, we all like hearing a little gossip. "The problem is, we don't necessarily like—and we definitely don't respect—the people who dish that dirt," Haden says. Don't laugh at other people. When you do, the people around you wonder if you sometimes laugh at them.

...But Readily Admit Your Failings

Be humble. Share your screw-ups. Admit your mistakes. Be the cautionary tale. And laugh at yourself. "While you should never laugh at other people, you should always laugh at yourself," Haden says. "People will like you better for it—and they'll want to be around you a lot more."

ATTENTION, INTROVERTS

One of the most persistent stereotypes within entrepreneurship is that founders must be true extroverts: gregarious, outgoing, and always ready to press the flesh. If the image of glad-handing your way through a crowd sets your teeth on edge, you might assume that running a business is not for you.

If so, put that thought out of your mind. According to Sophia Dembling, author of *The Introvert's Way: Living a Quiet Life in a Noisy World*, introverts not only can be effective in business, but they also have traits that support good leadership. The important thing is to understand how to make your psychology work for what you want.

WHAT IS AN INTROVERT, REALLY?

The first step is to realize that shyness and introversion are not the same. "As one researcher explained it to me, shyness is a behavior in reaction to conditions, and introversion is a motivation," Dembling says. Natural extroverts can actually be shy. Whether introvert or extrovert, it's important to know that shyness can be overcome. "Introversion is hardwired, and there is no reason to want to overcome it," she says.

As Dembling describes it, introverts lose energy from being around people and gain energy from being alone, while extroverts are the opposite. "It's simply a different way of functioning in the world and no better or worse than extroversion, although we've all been told that extroversion is better," she says.

HOW TO WORK WITH WHAT YOU ARE

When you know how you best function, you can come up with tactics to take advantage of your inclinations. For example, if you must be at a conference and interact with many people, be sure to keep evenings free for some downtime by yourself. "Maybe you don't want to go to group events where you're trying to throw elevator pitches out," Dembling says. "Maybe you need to schedule one-on-one meetings." You might also look for odd moments to recharge during the day, whether that's taking a walk around the block or lunch by yourself.

Interestingly, public speaking may be fine if you can work from a prepared script or presentation and not improvise. "It's really recognizing where your strengths are and where your weaknesses are and not judging them," she says.

KEY DECISIONS TO CONSIDER

Being introverted will also affect strategic choices of how to structure your business. For example, an introverted business owner or executive might choose to lead a team of extroverts. "Your abilities to listen and process information are real strengths," Dembling says. "You might need to listen, step back, think about it, and come back to them," and avoid being steamrolled by team members. An extrovert might run into conflicts competing with extroverted team members, and be better off with a largely introverted team.

An introspective entrepreneur might favor a smaller business run out of a home office, with significant amounts of private time, rather than a larger undertaking, although it is possible to fall into the trap of isolating yourself too much.

Because of the confusion with shyness or its opposite—boldness—you might want to get a better sense of where you fall on the continuum between introversion and extroversion. Tests like the Myers-Briggs Type Indicator can provide an inexact approach to understanding where you might stand.

PRODUCTIVITY 101:
WHAT SUCCESSFUL LEADERS DO EVERY DAY

Now that we've outlined the characteristics of high-performing entrepreneurs, it's time to look at their unique habits.

Kevin Kruse, author of numerous business books, interviewed over two hundred ultra-successful people, including seven billionaires, thirteen Olympians, and a host of accomplished entrepreneurs. One of his most revealing sources of information came from their answers to a simple open-ended question: "What is your number one secret to productivity?"

In analyzing their responses, Kruse found some fascinating suggestions. Try them out and see where they take you.

Focus on minutes, not hours. Most people default to hour and half-hour blocks on their calendar; highly successful people know that there are 1,440 minutes in every day and that there is nothing more valuable than time. Money can be lost and made again, but time spent can never be reclaimed. As Olympic gymnast Shannon Miller told Kruse, "To this day, I keep a schedule that is almost *minute by minute.*" You must master your minutes to master your life.

Focus on only one thing. Ultra-productive people know what their most important task is and work on it for one to two hours each morning, *without interruptions*. What task will have the biggest impact on reaching your goals? What accomplishment will get you promoted at work? That's what you should dedicate your mornings to every day.

Don't use to-do lists. Throw away your to-do list; instead, schedule everything on your calendar. It turns out that only 41 percent of items on to-do lists ever get done. All those undone items lead to stress and insomnia because of the Zeigarnik effect, which, in essence, means that uncompleted tasks will stay on your mind until you finish them. Highly productive people put everything on their calendar and then work and live by that calendar.

Beat procrastination with time travel. Your future self can't be trusted. That's because we are *time inconsistent*. We buy veggies today because we think we'll eat healthy salads all week; then we throw out green rotting mush in the future. Successful people figure out what they can do *now* to make certain their future selves will do the right thing. Anticipate how you will self-sabotage in the future, and come up with a solution today to defeat your future self.

Make it home for dinner. Kruse gleaned this one from Intel's Andy Grove, who said, "There is always more to be done, more that should be done, always more than can be done." Highly successful people know what they value in life. Yes, work, but also what *else* they value. There is no right answer, but for many, these other values include family time, exercise, and giving back. They consciously allocate their 1,440 minutes a day to each area they value (i.e., they put them on their calendar), and then they stick to that schedule.

Use a notebook. Richard Branson has said on more than one occasion that he wouldn't have been able to build Virgin without a simple notebook, which he takes with him wherever he goes. In one interview, Greek shipping magnate Aristotle Onassis said, "Always carry a notebook. Write everything down. That is a million-dollar lesson they don't teach you in business school!" Ultra-productive people free their minds by writing *everything* down as the thoughts come to them.

Process emails only a few times a day. Ultra-productive people don't check their email throughout the day. They don't respond to each vibration or ding to see who has intruded into their inbox. Instead, like everything else, they *schedule* time to process their emails quickly and efficiently. For some, that's only once a day; for others, it's morning, noon, and night.

Avoid meetings at all costs. When Kruse asked Mark Cuban to give his best productivity advice, he quickly responded, "Never take meetings unless someone is writing a check." Meetings are notorious time killers. They start late, have the wrong people in them, meander around their topics, and run long. You should get out of meetings whenever you can and hold fewer of them yourself. If you *do* run a meeting, keep it short and to the point.

Say *no* to almost everything. Billionaire Warren Buffett once said, "The difference between successful people and very successful people is that very successful people say *no* to almost everything." And self-help guru James Altucher colorfully gave Kruse this tip: "If something is not a *Hell Yeah!* then it's a *no*." Remember, you only have 1,440 minutes in a day. Don't give them away easily.

Follow the 80/20 rule. Known as the Pareto Principle, in most cases, 80 percent of results come from only 20 percent of activities. Ultra-productive people know which activities drive the greatest results. Focus on those and ignore the rest.

Delegate almost everything. Ultra-productive people don't ask, "How can I do this task?" Instead, they ask, "How can this task get done?" They take the *I* out of it as much as possible. Ultra-productive people don't have control issues, and they are not micro-managers. In many cases, good enough is, well, good enough.

Touch things only once. How many times have you opened a piece of regular mail—a bill perhaps—and then put it down, only to deal with it again later? How often do you read an email and then close it and leave it in your inbox to deal with later? Highly successful people try to "touch it once." If it takes less than five or ten minutes—whatever it is—they deal with it right then and there. It reduces stress, since it won't be in the back of their minds, and it is more efficient, since they won't have to reread or reevaluate the item in the future.

Practice a consistent morning routine. Kruse's single greatest surprise while interviewing over two hundred highly successful people was how many of them wanted to share their morning ritual with him. While he heard about a wide variety of habits, most nurtured their bodies in the morning with water, a healthy breakfast, and light exercise, and they nurtured their minds with meditation or prayer, inspirational reading, or journaling.

Understand that energy is everything. You can't make more minutes in the day, but you can increase your energy to increase your attention, focus, and productivity. Highly successful people don't skip meals, sleep, or breaks in the pursuit of more, more, more. Instead, they view food as fuel, sleep as recovery, and breaks as opportunities to recharge in order to get even more done.

You might not be an Olympian or a billionaire (yet), but their secrets just might help you become more productive and successful.

Now that we've defined the qualities of exceptional leadership, and given you tips on how to be more productive, it's time to take the world by storm. In the following pages, we'll look at the growth strategies you can use to take your startup to the next level.

PREPARE TO GO GLOBAL

" When entrepreneurs come to me for advice, I tell them to keep two things in mind. One, always build a business to last forever. And two, build the business so that it can be sold for as much money as possible even if selling is not part of the plan."

NORM BRODSKY, serial entrepreneur and *Inc.*'s "Street Smarts" columnist.

THIS LAST CHAPTER WILL FOCUS on growth—essentially, turning your small business into a big one. In other words, world domination.

Disclaimer: We're using that term loosely. We don't necessarily mean your product or service *needs* to be all over the globe. That said, as the planet grows smaller, you may want to consider dipping your toe into international waters. (More on that later in the chapter.)

Instead, this chapter outlines common growth strategies to take your business to the next level.

"Turning a small business into a big one is never easy," says Darren Dahl, a contributing editor at *Inc.* "The statistics are grim." Research suggests that only one-tenth of 1 percent of companies will ever reach $250 million in annual revenue. An even more microscopic group, just 0.036 percent, will reach $1 billion in annual sales.

In other words, most businesses start small and stay there.

But if that's not good enough for you—or if you recognize that staying small doesn't necessarily guarantee your business's survival—

there are examples of companies out there that have successfully made the transition from startup to small business to fully thriving large business.

Keith McFarland, an entrepreneur and former Inc. 500 CEO, researched how small companies pushed past the entrepreneurial phase for his book, *The Breakthrough Company.* "There have always been lots of books out there on how to run a big company," says McFarland, who now runs his own consulting business, McFarland Partners, based in Salt Lake City. But he couldn't find one about how to push a startup to major-player status. "So I studied the companies that had done it to learn their lessons," he says.

What follows is what McFarland learned, which anyone seeking to grow his or her business can use.

INTENSIVE GROWTH STRATEGIES

Part of getting from A to B is to put together a growth strategy that McFarland says, "brings you the most results from the least amount of risk and effort." Growth strategies resemble a kind of ladder, where lower-level rungs present less risk but maybe less quick-growth impact. The bottom line for small businesses, especially startups, is to focus on those strategies that are at the lowest rungs of the ladder and then gradually move your way up as needed. As you go about developing your growth strategy, you should first consider the lower rungs of what are known as "intensive growth strategies." Each new rung brings more opportunities for fast growth, but also more risk. They are:

1. **Market penetration.** The least risky growth strategy for any business is to simply sell more of its current product to its current customers—a strategy perfected by large consumer goods companies, says McFarland. Think of how you might buy a six-pack of beverages, then a twelve-pack, and then a case. "You can't even buy toilet paper in anything less than a twenty-four-roll pack these days," McFarland jokes. Finding new ways for your customers to use your product—like turning baking soda into a deodorizer for your refrigerator—is another form of market penetration.

2. **Market development.** The next rung up the ladder is to devise a way to sell more of your current product to an adjacent market—offering your product or service to customers in another city or state, for example. McFarland points out that many of the great fast-growing companies of recent decades relied on market development as their main growth strategy. For example, Express Personnel (now called Express Employment Professionals), a staffing business that began in Oklahoma City, quickly opened offices around the country via a franchising model. Eventually, the company offered employment staffing services in more than 770 different locations, generating $3 billion in sales in 2016.

3. **Alternative channels.** This growth strategy involves pursuing customers in a different way. For example, selling your products online. When Apple added its retail division,

it was also adopting an alternative channel strategy. Using the Internet as a means for your customers to access your products or services in a new way, such as by adopting a rental model or software as a service, is another alternative channel strategy.

4. **Product development.** A classic strategy, it involves developing new products to sell to your existing customers as well as to new ones. (For more on staying innovative, see Chapter 5.) If you have a choice, you would ideally like to sell your new products to existing customers. That's because selling products to your existing customers is far less risky than "having to learn a new product and market at the same time," McFarland says.

5. **New products for new customers.** Sometimes, market conditions dictate that you must create new products for new customers, as Polaris, the recreational vehicle manufacturer in Minneapolis, found out. For years, the company produced only snowmobiles. Then, after several mild winters, the company was in dire straits. Fortunately, it developed a wildly successful series of four-wheel all-terrain vehicles, opening up an entirely new market. Similarly, Apple pulled off this strategy when it introduced the iPod. What made the iPod such a breakthrough product was that it could be sold alone, independent of an Apple computer, but at the same time it helped expose more new customers to the computers Apple offered. McFarland says the iPhone has had a similar im-

pact; once customers began to enjoy the look and feel of the product's interface, they opened themselves up to buying other Apple products.

If you choose to follow one of the intensive growth strategies, you should ideally take only one step up the ladder at a time, since each step brings risk, uncertainty, and effort. The rub is that, sometimes, the market forces you to take action as a means of self-preservation, as it did with Polaris. Sometimes, you have no choice but to take more risk, says McFarland.

INTEGRATIVE GROWTH STRATEGIES

If you've exhausted all steps along the intensive growth strategy path, you can then consider growth through acquisition or integrative growth strategies. The problem is that some 75 percent of all acquisitions fail to deliver on the value or efficiencies predicted for them. In some cases, a merger can end in total disaster (let us not forget the AOL-Time Warner deal in 2000). Nevertheless, there are three viable choices when it comes to implementing an integrative growth strategy. They are:

1. **Horizontal.** This growth strategy would involve buying a competing business or businesses. Employing such a strategy not only adds to your company's growth, it also eliminates another barrier standing in the way of future growth—namely, a real or potential competitor. Compa-

nies such as Paychex, the payroll services provider, and Intuit, the maker of personal and small business tax and accounting software, acquired key competitors over the years as both a shortcut to product development and as a way to increase their share of the market.

2. **Backward.** A backward integrative growth strategy would involve buying one of your suppliers as a way to better control your supply chain. Doing so could help you to develop new products faster and potentially more cheaply. For instance, Fastenal, a company based in Winona, Minnesota, that sells nuts and bolts (among other things), made the decision to acquire several tool and die makers as a way to introduce custom-part manufacturing capabilities to its larger clients.

3. **Forward.** Acquisitions can also be focused on buying component companies that are part of your distribution chain. For instance, if you were a garment manufacturer like Chicos, which is based in Fort Myers, Florida, you could begin buying up retail stores as a means to pushing your product at the expense of your competition.

DIVERSIFICATION

Another category of growth strategies that was popular in the 1950s and 1960s and is used far less often today is something called diversification, where you grow your company by buying another company that is completely unrelated to your business. Massive conglomerates such as General Electric are essentially holding companies for a diverse range of businesses based solely on their financial performance. That's how GE could have a nuclear power division, a railcar manufacturing division, and a financial services division all under the letterhead of a single company. This kind of growth strategy tends to be fraught with risk and problems, says McFarland, and is rarely considered viable these days.

HOW WILL YOU GROW?

Growth strategies are never pursued in a vacuum, and being willing to change course in response to feedback from the market is as important as implementing a strategy in a single-minded way. Too often, companies take a year to develop a strategy and, by the time they're ready to implement it, the market has changed on them, says McFarland. That's why, when putting together a growth strategy, he advises companies to think in just ninety-day chunks. Sometimes the best approach is to take it one rung at a time.

MANAGING RISK

Whatever strategy you choose, growing a small company will entail some level of risk.

"As a smart entrepreneur, you don't let this stop you from weighing the facts and making the best possible choices," says Rhett

Power, co-founder of the toy company Wild Creations. And if your expansion doesn't go as planned? "You develop a new strategy from a wiser perspective," he suggests.

> " The biggest risk is not taking any risk. In a world that's changing really quickly, the only strategy that is guaranteed to fail is not taking risks."
>
> **MARK ZUCKERBERG,** founder of Facebook

When you have limited resources and narrow profit margins, learning how to manage risk should be a top priority. Here is how Power recommends doing it:

→ **Track your cash flow.** How much money do you have right now? Can you pay your bills? What if your biggest client went elsewhere? Ideally, you have three to six months of funds tucked away to cover expenses. Be conservative. Ask your vendors for sixty or ninety days to pay. You should always know your financial status, good or bad, and have a realistic contingency plan—especially before making big moves.

→ **Listen to warnings.** If you've hired well, or have close advisors, you can trust their doubts. Are they seeing something concerning in a contract, employee, vendor—or in your growth strategy itself? It's easy to dismiss others' opinions, but you need to listen. "They have your best interest at heart, even if you don't want to hear it," Power says. "Thank them and reward them."

→ **Get legal.** You can't grow and succeed without legal advice. Have an attorney review your contracts, the terms of your deals, and even the structure of your company. "Yes, it costs money, but you can't afford *not* to protect yourself," Power says. Hire an accountant to help you manage cash flow and get a handle on your company's numbers. Chances are that, at some point, you will be glad you had the foresight to hire professionals.

→ **Avoid commitment.** It may feel secure to, say, sign a long-term office lease. Until you are firmly established, you need to be nimble and able to make quick adjustments. Clients change and projects go sideways. You may decide to narrow your focus...or expand it. Something like an expensive address can become a detriment. Whatever it is, be cautious about committing to anything that could be a drain on your finances.

Risk is necessary. In fact, "it can be exhilarating to take you to the next level," Power says. "Remember, Mark Zuckerberg wouldn't have succeeded without risk." But always, even when you become an Inc. 500 company, manage that risk carefully.

Risky Businesses

 Here are a few businesses that took risks to grow—and it paid off.

- **Microsoft.** The story of Microsoft is long and varied and riddled with missteps, especially when it comes to mobile devices. But back in 2001, the tech giant pushed the envelope with its first gaming console: the Xbox. At a time when it seemed like there could be no rival to the Playstation, the company doubled down on their marketing budget for the device. Now, the Xbox isn't just a way to play games, it's also a major player when it comes to "Over the Top" television and video streaming.

- **Google.** Once upon a time, there was no Google. Co-founders Larry Page and Sergey Brin created the company while Ph.D. students at Stanford University, and almost gave up on it all because it was taking way too much time. Page nearly sold the company in 1997 for just $1.5 million. Later on in 2006, when no one understood the potential of a little video service called YouTube, the tech company bought it up. The rest is history.

- **TOMS.** When Blake Mycoskie founded TOMS, many investors laughed at the business model *and* the fashion. Mycoskie went all in, though, starting and running the business from the very beginning. Not only has TOMS launched multiple product lines, but the "buy one, give one" concept has defined an entire generation of millennial consumers and the sharing economy.

- **Whole Foods.** Remember when buying organic and natural products seemed like a fancy idea? You can blame these four food lovers from Texas—John Mackey and Renee Lawson Hardy, owners of Safer Way Natural Foods, and Craig Weller and Mark Skiles, owners of Clarksville Natural Grocery—for the rise of the all-natural economy. They all left their popular shopping market gigs to bet on Whole Foods, which could have been a major flop. But by believing in the model, and starting out with just nineteen employees in 1980, they've changed the entire culture of grocery shopping and food preparation.

- **Intel.** The foundational company of everything digital, Intel announced plans in 2016 to reinvent itself, ditching some of its chips and concentrating on server systems and the cloud. They're betting it all on the Internet of Things. Whether the risk really will pay off in the end, still remains to be seen.

MM.LaFleur

IN 2014, SARAH LAFLEUR was facing the prospect that her women's clothing brand, MM.LaFleur, might go out of business. When the New York City–based company did trunk shows, customers—mostly working women who wanted to dress well but abhorred shopping—typically returned for a second purchase. But when it came to MM.LaFleur's primary business, e-commerce, it couldn't figure out how to recruit new customers.

So, LaFleur's team decided to experiment: They emailed their most loyal shoppers and asked if the company could send them a box of clothing selected for them by a stylist. More than 18 percent opted in.

Today, the Bento Boxes, as they're called, account for 80 percent of the company's new sales, and since they were launched, 40 percent of first-time customers return within twelve weeks to make another purchase. MM.LaFleur has now stepped back from the precipice and is on track to pull in more than $70 million in 2017.

LaFleur thought up the growth idea thanks to her childhood in Japan, where she packed multicompartment bento lunches for school. The company's bentos are similar, with layered boxes separating clothes and accessories. It's cheeky, but also highly functional: The design helps the clothes arrive unwrinkled. The garments come packed neatly in reusable, zippered plastic bags—a small but practical luxury, according to customers who repurpose them to store gym clothes or to separate items in a suitcase.

The company is also employing other growth strategies. After testing a brick-and-mortar showroom in New York City, MM.LaFleur found that women who booked appointments there often spent up to three times more than online-only shoppers. So in 2016 it opened a permanent showroom in Washington, D.C., and has long-term pop-ups planned for Boston and other locations around the country. Women get free one-hour sessions with personal stylists who select clothing for them ahead of time, along with bottomless glasses of Prosecco. "We do our best to communicate over email," says LaFleur. "But nothing replicates the offline service."

HOW TO DELEGATE

" The surest way for an executive to kill himself is to refuse to learn how, and when, and to whom to delegate work."

—

JAMES CASH PENNEY, founder of the J.C. Penney retail chain

Here's something many startup entrepreneurs forget: If you truly want to scale your business, you'll need to learn how to delegate so you can focus on your company's bigger picture issues.

"As organizations grow increasingly complex, duties and responsibilities across the workforce can become less well defined," writes Robert Heller in *How to Delegate*. "Often it seems as though everyone is doing everyone else's job. Delegation is the manager's key to efficiency, and benefits all."

But delegating isn't the simple, straightforward process it masquerades as; it takes time and effort to master the art.

"The inability to delegate properly is the main reason that executives fail," says Harvey Mackay, who founded Mackay Envelope Company, now MackayMitchell Envelope Company, in 1959. He remembers needing to hire a person to run the company's day-to-day operations while he studied the industry and charted his company's future direction. "I learned quickly that delegating often requires a detour outside your comfort zone."

Managers often mistake delegation for passing off work. "So they don't do it—and they wind up wasting their time as well as the company's time and resources," Mackay says.

How do you start delegating successfully? Here are some tips.

1. **Don't look for perfection.** Your objective is to get the job done, not create a masterpiece. Establish a standard of quality and a fair time frame for reaching it. Once you establish the expectations, let your staff decide how to carry out the project. "You have to learn to trust your staff," says Larry Alton, an independent business consultant. "You're the one that hired them—isn't that because you thought they were good at their jobs?" Yes, you might challenge them with some tasks outside their comfort zones, but you'll be there to guide them if they run into any trouble along the way.

2. **Provide complete job instructions.** Make sure your employee has all the information needed to complete the job. Confirm that "the members of your team understand the responsibilities you are asking them to take on," says Peter Economy, author of numerous business books. "Encourage them to ask questions if they are uncertain what it is you want them to do."

3. **Stop believing you're the only one who can do the job properly.** The biggest obstacle to successful delegation is the persistent urge to not delegate anything at all. Sometimes, it's a point of pride for a boss to retain as much work as possible. "But more often, it's created from the mentality that your workers wouldn't be able to handle it, or that they wouldn't get it done the right way," Alton says. Just

because an employee does things differently doesn't mean he or she won't do the job right or as well. "If you establish expectations of the goal and the standards to follow, then methodology shouldn't be an issue," Mackay says. An important and often overlooked part of delegation is that it helps develop employees for advancement and creates a better work environment.

4. **Focus on teaching new skills.** Though the assignment of your first few tasks will take more time than it will save you (since you'll need to train your chosen employee), consider it an investment. By transferring those skills, you'll be opening the door to assigning similar tasks to that individual in the future, ultimately saving more time than you spent teaching. And don't forget: As you hand over greater responsibility, it's important to understand that learning new skills sometimes includes making mistakes. "Don't punish employees who make a good-faith effort to do things right," Mackay says.

5. **Check on progress.** Let the employee do the work, but check in periodically on progress. Don't look over employees' shoulders or watch their every move. When you outline the expectations in the beginning, make sure you build in checkpoints for follow-up. "When you check your employees' work, not only will you catch issues and problems as they occur, but also your employees will be motivated by your personal attention to the work they are doing," Economy says.

6. **Say thank you to the people who have accepted the responsibility.** If your workers have done well with a task you assigned, let them know by publicly thanking them and offering genuine praise. If they've fallen short, don't be afraid to give them some constructive criticism.

HOW TO GO GLOBAL

When you ask CEOs of small-to-mid-sized companies how they intend to grow, they generally cite innovation—coming up with new products for existing markets or winning market share from competitors. And they cite acquisition. Far fewer mention expanding internationally.

But these days, many companies can tap into a new revenue stream by selling their existing products to entirely new customers in global markets. Lower travel costs and easier communications have made it significantly easier to do so.

"Going global can be scary. Really scary. You can easily get in over your head," says Melissa Lamson, a business consultant. "But the more homework you do, the lower the risk. And, I can assure you the rate of return can be huge."

The U.S. Small Business Administration, which estimates that only 1 percent of small businesses are currently exporting overseas, urges entrepreneurs to take their products worldwide. Some 96 percent of all of the world's consumers and over three-quarters of the world's purchasing power are outside of the United States, according to the SBA.

"India and China add an Australia and New Zealand to their populations every year," says Suresh Kumar, who has served on the United States National Export Initiative. "How can you afford to ignore those? That's where the markets are gravitating."

We asked a few experts for their best tips on tapping world markets. Here's what they said.

1. **Choose your overseas markets with care.** The first step in expanding internationally is to pinpoint the country or region you want to expand into. You need to base these decisions largely on cultural, economic, and political factors, as well as on market risk—and on where there are potential customers for your goods and services. For instance, take a look at where international traffic or orders are originating from on your website. When considering a country, find out whether there are any tariffs on your products or trade barriers, and understand the economic and political policy of the country.

2. **Conduct market research.** "Speak with customers, marketing partners, or distributors and evaluate competitive products," advises Lamson. For research, you might start with the Department of Commerce's website or TradePort.org, a repository of information for businesses conducting trade. The types of research you can do include primary market research—collecting data directly from international marketplaces through telephone interviews or contacting potential customers or government representatives. Your research can also include secondary mar-

ket research, such as news articles, trade statistics, and data from export specialists.

3. **Put boots on the ground.** There is no replacement for having a member of your team on the ground and experiencing the specific international market, getting close to the customer, and checking out the competition, says Marc Meyer, a professor of entrepreneurship at Northeastern University. "This is firsthand research," he says. "Once that's done, you can prototype anywhere, but your product or service must be tested directly with your target global customer."

4. **Know your enemy.** Take a deep dive into the market-specific competitive arena, understand the strengths and weaknesses of future challengers, and decide if there's a market opportunity for your product or service, Meyer says. "And, by all means, make sure your nomenclature translates properly in the new market," he adds. A number of big companies have made classic blunders, such as Mercedes-Benz entering China under the brand name "Bensi," which literally translated means "rush to die." The same goes for a logo: A crown, for instance, may have different meanings, depending on the country.

5. **Alter your pricing model as you learn.** The dynamics of distribution, pricing, and packaging tend to be very different for foreign markets. In India, for example, it's largely about high volume and low price; China is high volume but a broader product portfolio; and the Gulf States, low volume, but premium. In many global markets, the distribution

structure is very different than the United States, Meyer says, meaning you need to become an expert in how to sell within an international target.

6. **Ask for help.** One of the mistakes business owners can make is being too solo-minded in their thinking about new markets, says Minas Apelian, a vice president in external venturing at Saint Gobain, a French multinational corporation. Create a comprehensive list of companies in your industry, visit their websites, and reach out to their executive teams. You may find partnership opportunities here, in addition to creating alliances. Also review country-specific industry association websites and begin connecting with the leaders or executive boards of those organizations. Likewise, research industry-related trade shows and follow the same process of meeting the organizers and learning about your industry in that region. Any of these moves "can provide a small business owner with the where, when, and how to enter, say, Brazil, without investing precious time and money," he says. Caution, he adds, is the watchword.

7. **Test. Learn. Refine.** Do all of your product or service testing, learning, and refining here in the United States before contemplating a foreign foray, Apelian advises. "Make your mistakes here," he says. "Learn from them. Then begin conducting due diligence on a target market."

8. **Devise an export strategy.** Your prospects for selling overseas will be helped if you put together an export plan that details your business goals, your plan for financing

this expansion, and how you intend to sell your goods or services abroad. One of the key questions you need to ask is how you are going to sell your goods overseas. Building an international sales team can be achieved through partnerships, alliances, and direct hiring. You may also want to research local executive recruiters, local and niche job boards, and the local newspapers to learn more about how talent in that particular region finds the best employers. If you plan to sell online, you can simply let the international customers find your website and shop just as your domestic customers already do. Using this method, you still need to figure out how to ship overseas and learn about foreign taxes, duties, and customs laws. You can also actively find ways of using your website to target new foreign markets. This might include translating parts of your website into a local language, and employing a fluent speaker to use social networks to attract interest in your website, business, and products or services.

9. **Accept local business customs, don't fight them.** Every market will have local ways of doing things that are different from what you know, says Ian Jackson, managing partner with consultancy Enshored, who has led global businesses. "There have been times I've been utterly frustrated at how long it takes to do some things or how much things cost in some markets," he says. "But you are a foreigner and as much as you think you know better, the locals don't need to hear it." Going along with the local customs is the better approach.

<<<<<< **CASE STUDY** >>>>>>

99 Designs

"GOING GLOBAL" IS MUCH easier said than done. That's according to Patrick Llewellyn, the CEO of 99 Designs, an online graphic design marketplace based in San Francisco with offices in Melbourne, Berlin, Paris, London, and Rio de Janeiro.

"A startup that wants to go global has to build trust in each new market *locally*," he says. Customers respond to companies that provide a service tailored to their needs, so localization is essential. "But it's both time-consuming and expensive."

Llewellyn says the company, founded in 2008, still thinks like a bootstrapped startup, which has helped it expand its reach. "We've managed to go global while using a minimum of resources," he says.

For companies interested in entering a foreign market, Llewellyn says the minimal starting point is a website on a regional domain operating in the local language. Your next step should be to hire one support person to give you feedback about local customers' desires, or their complaints, he says. (99 Designs uses freelancing sites such as Upwork to hire native speakers; it also hires local public relations and marketing professionals on a contractual basis.) "You can hold off on other aspects of localization, such as offering adapted payment options, while you are building your initial presence," he says. "But you do need that crucial element of a person fluent in the local language and culture who can relay feedback."

Another way to enter a market affordably is to acquire a smaller business that already has local traction and presence. "This gives you both market entry and instant local reference data to test against and, unlike just opening an office, it also creates a newsworthy event," Llewellyn says. "There are obvious PR, social media, and SEO benefits to that kind of event, but just as importantly it shows your commitment to the region or country."

Once you've expanded, Llewellyn recommends managing that market locally. "Our one major hire in each new market we enter is a country manager," he says. "We then ask that person to treat their operation as its own mini-startup." The country managers drive strategy, head up marketing, create events, and perform all ongoing local translation, he says. That way, they are truly immersed in that market. "They're able to create an authentic tone with customers because they understand both the region and our business," he says.

Finally, Llewellyn says 99 Designs relies on a variety of

communications tools to keep its far-flung teams together, including Dropbox, Slack, and Basecamp. The company also uses Trello for project management, Blue Jeans for videoconferencing, Atlassian Confluence for information sharing, Geckoboard for dashboards, and Google Docs for real-time collaboration. "We also use Smartling, a translation management platform that lets us quickly launch versions of our site in different languages, while controlling costs around translation," he says.

Going global is costly in terms of time, money, and focus. But it's an effective way to grow a business, as long as you develop a strong connection with your new market, Llewellyn says.

—

>>>> **CONCLUSION**

SO WHY DO IT?
We sometimes ask that question when we interview entrepreneurs. We want to know why they put so much on the line, why they sacrifice so much time away from family, and, above all, why they work so damn hard. It seems a heck of a lot easier to work for someone else and get a steady paycheck (and maybe sick time, paid vacation, and benefits, too).

Granted, we feature many success stories on *Inc.*'s cover or homepage and it's likely easy for a person who has achieved fantastical fame or fortune to wax poetic about the joys of entrepreneurship.

But keep in mind, our reporters and editors talk to people at all stages of business ownership. So we hear a little bit about the struggle. Actually, we hear a *lot* about the struggle. We hear about fights with zoning boards, meltdowns of computer systems, and nightmares about not making payroll. We know that running a business entails putting out a lot of fires, both figurative and literal.

Yet, we still hear excitement in people's voices—even on the difficult days—when we ask them about what made them start their own business. "I always wanted to be able to call my own shots, be in charge of my destiny, and have the ability to set my own life," one entrepreneur told *Inc.* Another spoke of never "going back to corporate and being a robot again." Still others have told us that they were motivated to start a company to forge a lasting legacy.

We've heard it all. Women entrepreneurs tell us that they were drawn to starting a company because they could have more control over their schedules than in the corporate world. (It's perhaps not a news flash that women are still the primary caretakers of children and elderly family members.) Immigrant entrepreneurs, and people of color, tell us they wanted to launch a business because they saw opportunities that no one else was chasing. The formerly incarcerated tell us they were motivated to do their own thing because absolutely no one else would hire them. Extroverts say they want to start a business because that's what extroverts do. Introverts say they want to start a business because they don't like working for extroverts. And the list goes on.

You'll have your own reasons for starting your own company—and whatever they are, we hope the advice, insight, and stories we've shared in these pages will help you in your own entrepreneurial journey. We've rarely heard anyone say they've regretted giving entrepreneurship a shot. But we do hear a lot of people saying: "I really wish I had taken that idea and run with it." Now get going.